MAK SENSE OF BUSINESS

*In memory of my grandmother
Edna Bucknall, 1911 – 2007*

MAKING SENSE OF BUSINESS

A no-nonsense guide to business skills
for managers and entrepreneurs

ALISON BRANAGAN

KOGAN PAGE

London and Philadelphia

Publisher's note

Every possible effort has been made to ensure that the information contained in this book is accurate at the time of going to press, and the publishers and author cannot accept responsibility for any errors or omissions, however caused. No responsibility for loss or damage occasioned to any person acting, or refraining from action, as a result of the material in this publication can be accepted by the editor, the publisher or the author.

First published in Great Britain and the United States in 2009 by Kogan Page Limited

120 Pentonville Road
London N1 9JN
United Kingdom
www.koganpage.com

525 South 4th Street, #241
Philadelphia PA 19147
USA

© Alison Branagan, 2009
© Tim Bradford (illustrations) 2009

ISBN 978 0 7494 5486 9

British Library Cataloguing-in-Publication Data

A CIP record for this book is available from the British Library.

Library of Congress Cataloging-in-Publication Data

Branagan, Alison.
  Making sense of business : a no-nonsense guide to business skills for managers and entrepreneurs / Alison Branagan.
    p. cm.
  Includes index.
  ISBN 978-0-7494-5486-9
  1. Entrepreneurship. 2. New business enterprises--Management. 3. Management.
I. Title.
  HD62.5.B725 2009
  658.1'1--dc22
                                    2009000748

Typeset by Saxon Graphics Ltd, Derby
Printed and bound in India by Replika Press Pvt Ltd.

Contents

About the author — viii

Foreword — ix

Acknowledgements — x

Introduction — 1

1. **What is enterprise?** — 4
   Business knowledge versus enterprise skills — 5
   What are enterprise skills? — 7

2. **Understanding risk** — 10
   Judging risk — 11
   How to analyse risk — 12

3. **Managing enterprising minds** — 18
   Managing a team-enterprise — 19
   Team-enterprise and risk management — 20
   Minimizing the risk of failure — 21

4. **How to focus** — 25
   How do you gain focus? — 26
   Vision — 29
   Goals — 31
   Achieving team goals — 34

5. **The importance of networking** — 38
   Why network? — 40
   Social networks — 42
   Beyond the comfort zone — 46
   How to network — 48

6. **Knowing your customer**   **55**
    Who is your customer?   56
    Develop an inquiring mind   57
    Understanding the mind of customers   60
    Value to the customer   62

7. **How to sell**   **67**
    The sales process   67
    How to structure a sales pitch   69
    Practical things to think about   71
    Customer not happy?   73

8. **Managing time wisely**   **79**
    How time is used   81
    Valuing time   82
    The business cake theory   83
    Seven segments of business time   87

9. **Legal and ethical matters**   **94**
    Crime   96
    Ethics   97
    Risks and insurance   99
    Intellectual and industrial property   100
    Contracts   104
    Other important laws   105
    Tax   107

10. **How to present yourself**   **111**
    Seven steps to successful presentation   111
    Improving daily communication   121

11. **Negotiation**   **125**
    Preparation   127
    Principles   128
    Tactics   131
    Presentation   134
    Seven steps to successful negotiation   136

12. **Keeping positive**   **145**
    Mindset   145
    Environment   146
    Dealing with rejection   149
    Cultivating a positive mindset   149

13. Creative thinking **155**
   Why is it needed? 155
   How is it cultivated? 156
   Being resourceful 159
   Creative problem solving 159
   Publicity stunts 163

14. Planning your next move **168**
   Goals and vision 169
   Importance of innovation and technology 170
   Managing growth 171
   In conclusion 174

   Glossary *177*
   Further reading *180*

About the author

Alison Branagan is a business consultant with a particular interest in creative fields, in which she is an experienced business adviser and lecturer.

Since 1998, she has studied different approaches to teaching business theory and enterprise skills. Many professional bodies have commissioned her to write web-based guides, speak at seminars and develop enterprise programmes for their members.

Over the last 10 years, she has established courses at a number of London universities, including Central Saint Martins College of Art and Design, and she conducts a series of master classes for the Association of Illustrators. She has also devised and facilitated upon many community enterprise projects for business and third-sector organizations.

She has a Master's degree in Applied Art and Visual Culture and is an ethical adviser for the AOI, an associate of the Institute of Business Consultants, a member of the Society of Authors and fellow of the Royal Society of Arts.

Foreword

Some are born business people, others have business thrust upon them. So, although I consider myself a designer and inventor first and foremost, I had no choice but to learn how to work in a business world.

There is an assumption that designers are hopeless at business but this is not tenable. Who understands the design, the manufacture and what it offers the user best? The designers, of course, so they are in pole position to understand the business.

When I started Dyson I made many mistakes. Now there's nothing wrong with that as it's how we learn and improve, but nevertheless, there are some I wish I'd avoided. For example, I lost the rights to one of my early inventions, the Ballbarrow, because of my inexperience of patent laws. This book will help you avoid such pitfalls by giving you practical examples and links to resources, not just theory.

There's also much to be said of the book's approach to clear communication. At Dyson we use simple sketches to share ideas. Alison's book mirrors this approach by using drawings to explain concepts and processes in a digestible way. As competition around the world intensifies, the need for good ideas is more important than ever, as is what to do with them next. Alison's book is the perfect place to start.

Sir James Dyson

Acknowledgements

I wish to thank the many friends and experts who have helped in the development of this book. First, I would like to thank Tim Bradford for his fantastic ability to transform my simple hand-drawn diagrams into entertaining illustrations.

Special thanks to consultants Trevor Burgess, John Foster, Karl Grupe, Roddy Mullin, Margaret Layton, Andrew Mallett, Peter Newby, David Stubbs, Peter Town, Silverman Sherliker LLP, Joan Yeadon and Albert Wright.

Thank you to the readers Yemisi Blake, Joan Branagan, Cecile Grant, Peter Hardisty and Adam Machin for their invaluable feedback.

For the chance to experiment with teaching enterprise programmes, acknowledgement must go to Kensington and Chelsea College, City University and Central Saint Martins College of Art and Design.

I would like to acknowledge inspiration for table 10.1 in chapter 10 from Presentation Skills Consultant Andrew Mallett, also Mind Gym publications (2005), Dorling Kindersley Essential Managers' series (Boulden, 2002 and Hindle, 1998) and Mike Southon and Chris West's *The Beermat Entrepreneur* (2002).

I would also like to thank Julia Swales, my commissioning editor at Kogan Page, for her guidance and patience.

Finally, I am indebted to John Naylor for his advice and consistent support.

Introduction

There is a multitude of business start-up books on the market today; very few approach the important subject of acquiring enterprise skills. This book is directed towards enterprising individuals and business managers who understand what they have to accomplish, but need to acquire new skills.

It could be the case that you are a student, or have recently set up a business. You may be curious about what enterprise skills are and wish to learn more about them. Equally, you may be a recent graduate applying for a managerial post in a small firm or perhaps already struggling in the deep end. Whatever the premise, the realization may have struck that the business or action plan now calls for application.

This book deals with practical activities and skills essential to achieve success. Acquiring such skills as selling, presentation and negotiation, among others, involves developing self-confidence and learning to work creatively. A special feature of *Making Sense of Business* is the explanation of theories with illustrated mind maps® and other creative exercises. These are to encourage fresh ways of thinking.

As you can see from thumbing through the book, you don't have to be an artist to draw out a simple plan using words, shapes and doodles. If you already possess creative flair, then use them as learning tools to help you think more strategically. Equally, they can be a useful visual aid to stimulate the imagination and improve problem-solving abilities. Making your own versions will be a valuable aide-memoire for any activity.

Why this book is called *Making Sense of Business*

- Do you sometimes think there is more to be gained from opportunities than other people suppose?
- Have you ever experienced that sinking feeling after meetings or presentations that, for some unfathomable reason, not all went to plan?
- Ever felt your performance could be improved?

This book will help by showing how to avoid making elementary mistakes by adopting creative approaches to business activities. The theories explored demonstrate how enterprise activities and skills are interrelated, and that business plans only work if applied practically.

The main issue when starting or developing any venture is the number of skills an entrepreneur needs to possess. No one who starts a business has all the knowledge and qualities desirable. To develop a business requires the assistance of talented individuals. Plenty of the most prosperous entrepreneurs and corporate tycoons have encountered more than a few problems during their careers.

Success in business is not just due to spirited persistence and overcoming initial failures. Successful entrepreneurs and senior managers think in different ways from the majority. I believe this is because they have a special ability to make connections between many factors at the same time. This is why visually planning a project is a useful exercise. It can provide an overview of all the issues and risks concerned, and further assist in identifying activities and resources.

To make money and achieve targets, owners and managers must acquire or hire people with different skills and expertise. For example, there is no advantage in devising an imaginative sales pitch if no one has the confidence to carry it off. There is equally no benefit in having good interpersonal skills if, after striking a deal, the contract is signed without a thorough understanding of its contents, and the agreement turns out later to be a bad one, full of loopholes and liabilities.

Why this book can help

This book covers:

- key enterprise theories and how to apply them;
- new ways to think about activities through mind mapping;

● creative exercises to help apply learning.

To get the best out of this book:

● Read each chapter and take a break before reading the next.
● You will realize that many subjects are interconnected, so it is advisable to make notes.
● Go back and re-read sections, think about them, and do the exercises.
● Completing the exercises is worth the effort, as they will improve thinking skills.
● Remember to make your own mind maps® as you go along.

1

What is enterprise?

Everyone lives by selling something.

Robert Louis Stevenson, novelist, 1850–1894

Some readers may view the word 'trade' as an old-fashioned term. To others it may sound fresh and contemporary, embracing 'free', 'fair' and 'global trade'. Enterprise is 'trading' in the sense of buying and selling goods, making and selling products, or simply selling services.

Trade is underpinned by two elements: 'business' theory in the form of knowledge, and practical 'enterprise' skills. Whether you are thinking of setting up a business or currently manage one, possessing both knowledge and skills are equally important. Enterprise skills help you 'apply' the 'theory' of business planning in the real world.

Enterprise

1. A project or undertaking, especially a *bold* one.
2. A business or company.

Oxford Concise Dictionary, 2006

If we look at a modern-day definition of 'enterprise' we see that it is a business initiative that requires being both 'bold' and 'resourceful'. The word 'enterprise' originates from the French root *'prendre'* meaning 'take', with the modern interpretation of 'something undertaken'. When looking through an older edition of the same dictionary, we meet with a similar description.

Enterprise

Undertaking, especially a bold or difficult one; courage, readiness to engage.

Oxford Concise Dictionary, 1934

Notice, 70 years earlier, the slightly more graceful definition included other words such as 'courage' and 'readiness to engage'. These explanations tell us that 'enterprise' is a risky affair, where one has to embrace chance with the confidence to act.

The opportunist

In the early 1960s, a teenager jumped off a Universal Studios' tour bus and wandered around the back lots. He met people who worked there and managed to gain access to the film studios where he watched professional film directors at work. He later squatted in an abandoned janitor's office, and used it to begin his adventure into the film industry. The young man in this story is Steven Spielberg, who incidentally was rejected from film school three times.

A large part of Steven Spielberg's enormous success is his willingness to take risks and make his own opportunities.

Business knowledge versus enterprise skills

Table 1.1 shows examples of how enterprise skills relate to business topics. If you are not familiar with both areas, 'knowledge' and 'skills', it is likely you will encounter problems. The best business plan in history will be truly worthless, if you don't have interpersonal skills or an enterprising mindset. Equally, charisma cannot compensate for lack of business knowledge. Some progress may be made by a loveable charmer, but failure to grasp the principles of business will inevitably lead to disaster. Business planning is just as important as running the shop.

The unprofitable business

I recall an engaging young man, who attended a number of my business seminars, who insisted that business plans are a waste of time. Since he started his enterprise, he had created many original products. This had

Table 1.1 Business and enterprise skills

Business	Enterprise
Essential theory or	Skills or approaches required for success.
Business plan	To make a theoretical plan a reality you must be able to focus, develop self-belief, and be determined.
Setting goals and	To achieve targets you require a vision, time management skills and the capacity to think positively.
Long-term objectives	Able to spot opportunities and having the flexibility to change direction.
Risk assessment	Being innovative and bold, judging risks and being willing to take them.
Research and	Able to understand customers, build contacts through networking and invest in innovation.
Market research	Knowing your customers, what they want and why. Being able to assess demand. Knowing how to make money from a business idea.
Marketing plan	How to sell, (when, where and how) sales pitch, presentation, promotion and PR.
Time management	Good self-management, delegation skills and working within deadlines.
Costing and pricing	How to value and make the best use of time and resources. Working out how to maximize profit.
Legal matters	Knowing how the law applies and trading legally.
Intellectual and	Understanding how to protect and commercially exploit intellectual property, such as trademarks, designs, artwork,
industrial property	brands and inventions, through registration and licensing.
Legal and money	Clear understanding of all the clauses in contracts, and having the confidence to negotiate a better deal.
Problem solving	Learning how to think creatively.
Continuous	Managing growth, expanding operations, and encouraging innovation.

fuelled his progress. However, after three years, his business simply was not making enough money. Underpinning this problem was a lack of business knowledge in terms of analysis and formal planning.

Entrepreneurial behaviour and character on their own can't sustain a commercial venture for long. Without drafting a basic business and financial plan, it is difficult to assess the feasibility and viability of a venture. The only way this micro-business owner would recover is to think through his problems. Otherwise, he will simply continue to run an unprofitable business.

Passion versus rationality

Many people choose to run a business for passionate reasons rather than rational ones. It is possible to get by with this approach to life, working long hours and days. However, to make a decent profit it is best to distance oneself and apply common sense to the situation. It is no good spending time on creating products or services that people don't want to buy, now or in the future; the sooner this is accepted the better. When you are emotionally involved with a business, commercial decisions can be difficult to make. **This is why learning more about business and enterprise skills is essential in order to make better decisions for the future.**

What are enterprise skills?

Table 1.1 demonstrates how theoretical business planning requires practical solutions. The enterprise skills listed are only suggestions; there are many other approaches to solving problems.

Entrepreneurs

There are other qualities and attributes associated with enterprising people. It is fair to argue that many entrepreneurs have naturally engaging personalities. In my experience of interviewing entrepreneurial characters over the years, I have found that many demonstrated a spirited rebelliousness from early childhood. I do believe that many people who start up a business are in fact unemployable. Many leaders and entrepreneurs tend to be overly adventurous, and test the boundaries well beyond the remit of an employee.

Enterprising managers

It is a very different proposition making decisions that affect the future of employees. When managing any kind of business there will always be periods of uncertainty. One of the main differences between the entrepreneur and the manager is that the former doesn't enjoy a regular salary. Therefore, managers do not incur the same degree of risk as business owners. However, the level of anxiety about achieving targets to maintain profits and increase job security could arguably be similar.

Managers contribute to the smooth running of the business, and are still directly responsible for the long-term interests of their teams or departments. Entrepreneurial behaviour among managers working within businesses is referred to as 'intrapreneurship' – meaning they can take risks within the limits of their responsibility. As we will discuss further later in this chapter, intrapreneurship is actively encouraged in modern innovative businesses.

Learning about how business works, making sense of it, will assist in making the right choices. Preparation combined with a bit of luck can lead to turning points for anyone.

Closing thoughts

Luck is what happens when preparation meets opportunity.

Seneca, Roman philosopher and statesman, 4 BC–65 AD

Thomas Jefferson, the third American president, famously proclaimed that he was a great believer in luck, and that the harder he worked the 'luckier' he became! Entrepreneurial success is dependent upon a number of qualities, characteristics and skills – hard work, luck and opportunity being important factors. However, inspiring leaders and intrapreneurial managers are viewed as intangible assets to a company. Whether as spirited mavericks or charismatic bosses, it's the atmosphere that they create which makes a difference. They nurture an enterprising outlook, inventing their own luck and opportunity.

Key points

- Always make an action or business plan before starting a venture.
- To put theory into practice will take time and require the mastering of new skills.
- Gain as much feedback as possible about a project and welcome constructive criticism.
- Be prepared for some rough and tumble in the early years.
- Make time for creativity and experimentation.
- Don't get too upset when things go wrong; it is part of the journey to achievement.

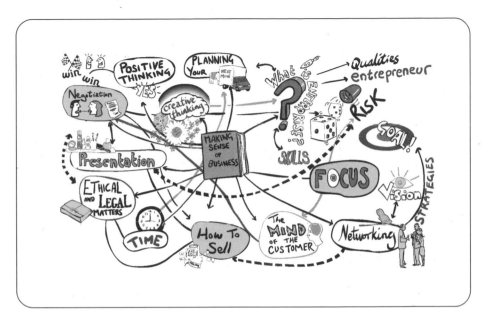

Enterprise skills booster

- What relatively simple business could you start tomorrow with £500 or US $1,000?
- Jot down a few ideas.
- Looking back, in the past was there an opportunity you would have liked to pursue but for some reason did not?
- Can you undertake this venture now?
- If not what would you like to do now?
- What new skills will you need to learn?
- How can you further your knowledge about this area of business or gain relevant work experience?
- Make a mind map® of selected thoughts and ideas.

Understanding risk

Where observation is concerned, chance favours only the prepared mindset.

Louis Pasteur, renowned chemist, 1822–1895

Risk

1. A situation involving exposure to danger.
2. The possibility that something unpleasant will happen.

Oxford Concise Dictionary, 2006

This modern definition of 'risk' reflects the Italian origins of the word, *'risco'* meaning 'danger'.

In business terminology, risk is about assessing the likelihood of failure: high, medium or low. Entrepreneurs and managers often have to take risks to thrive or survive – when starting new ventures nothing is certain. For instance, setting up a business, following the luxury of well-paid employment, can be a gamble. It is likely that earning a substantial return will take more than a few years' of hard work. However, if you disliked the day job, then a low income can be a small price to pay for freedom. It is a certainty that occasionally things will go wrong, money will be lost, bad decisions made and so on. The aim is to minimize or eliminate any threats you face by making good decisions.

Perception

It is important to understand that different people will evaluate the impact of risk in different ways. Attitudes to risk are related to perception and individual circumstance. For example from my research into this subject, I discovered that entrepreneurs from reasonably well-off backgrounds did not worry about taking risks, as they knew if things went wrong they had reserves to fall back on. And those who were less well off viewed risk with equal indifference, as they were so poor they felt they had nothing to lose!

Be willing to take risks

When starting or running a business, failure is a possibility. Many people decide not to start up a business because they fear things will go wrong. It's also worth considering the likelihood of the venture being a success. **Try not to let the thought of failure put you off from trying to do things.** These issues aside, the questions you should ask yourself are:

- First, if you don't take this risk, will you regret it in the future?
- Second, is not taking this risk a bigger risk than taking it?

Judging risk

October: This is one of the particularly dangerous months to invest in stocks; other dangerous months are July, January, September, April, November, May, March, June, December, August and February.

Mark Twain, humorist and writer, 1835–1910

The basics of risk assessment

There are huge tomes available in bookshops about risk assessment. It is a massive subject, which we will only touch upon here. From an elementary viewpoint, there are two types of risk, 'calculated' and 'stupid'. A decision about whether to proceed with a venture should be supported by thorough analysis and evaluation of your market research. It is also important to prioritize risks. This can only be achieved by thinking through in advance all the elements that could go wrong in a project or venture. Therefore, it is best to start by compiling a list of risks:

- What problems could occur?
- Which are most likely?
- Which ones would have the most serious impact?
- What can you do to mitigate them?

Thinking through risks can lead to positive improvements, and new ways of handling any difficulties.

How to analyse risk

To understand how to calculate risk, the following questions require consideration:

- What is likely to happen, personally and financially – and what will the impact be?
- What is the worst-case scenario – and what will the impact be?
- How will I minimize risks?
- If I can't minimize the risks, how can I manage them?

As you can understand from Table 2.1, risk calculation is about considering as many relevant factors as possible. Think about how the issues in the table will affect your business and reflect on how you can minimize or manage risks. In making decisions, one has to be bold and commit either way. In business, conditions fluctuate; being indecisive is not an option. If you are too slow to react, opportunities could be lost, or worse still, competitors might steal your market share.

Examples that may or may not affect your business

Table 2.1   Elements to consider in risk assessment

Theft	Not getting paid, being paid late	Working with others	Environmental laws	Hiring venues/ premises
Fire/flood	Running out of cash	No formal contract	Breaking a law	Change of weather
Accidents or injury caused	Poor costing and pricing	Agreeing to unfair contracts	Laws changing	Transport failure
Not having the correct (or any) insurance	Cancellation of orders	What if 'Mr X' suddenly died?	Government changing	Postal (or any kind of) strike
Damage to equipment	Rejection of products or services	Illness and general health problems	Ideas stolen, products copied	Stock/products broken before delivery
Computer failure	Losing mobile phone	Competence of others	Running out of cash	Crime wave
Recession/credit crunch	Aggressive competitors	Failure to keep up to date with technology	Staff leaving	Increase in interest/APR rates

In this matrix pick out factors that concern your business.

Examples of risk assessment

There are a number of factors to consider when assessing any situation.

- The worst-case end result for all questions 1, 2, 3 (below): 'I could possibly lose my house.'
- What is likely to happen for all questions 1, 2, 3: 'I would remortgage the house to cope with losses from misfortune.'

Q 1. If I do this thing, and it goes completely wrong, what will I lose?

To minimize risks I have undertaken thorough market research, and will not invest more than I can afford.

Scenario

It is likely 'A' may not happen, and possible 'B' will cancel.

To manage this risk, if 'A' fails I am willing to make contingency plans and find alternative options for 'B'.

Q 2. If I do this thing and I don't fully understand what it entails, what will I lose?

To minimize risks I will get my solicitor to read any contracts received in full, and ask them to explain everything to me in detail. I will also discuss this matter with trusted advisers to gain a number of viewpoints before finally agreeing the deal.

Scenario

It's possible that I might not be able to complete this undertaking in time.

To manage risk, I am prepared to cope with a degree of pressure. I have secure financial backing and reserves. I can also ask my friends to help or increase the size of my team to meet the deadline.

Q 3. If I do this thing and the law or regulations change, what will I lose?

To minimize risks I have spoken with my solicitor about up-and-coming legislation, checked national political parties' manifestos and policies at local government level.

Scenario

However, despite thorough checking, there was an unexpected election. The new government decided to bring in new laws, eg smoking ban, restricting immigration, which directly affects the profitability of the business.

To manage risk, the business can temporarily draw on reserves until we find a solution. The owner or manager may decide to quit the venture and pursue other options.

Calculated risks

Many areas of putting a business or action plan into practice have elements of risk taking attached to them. There are a few important questions to ask yourself:

- What do clients and customers desire?
- How much are clients or customers prepared to pay?
- Will the price or fee you plan to charge fit with the consumer's pocket?
- Will this venture work?
- How long will it take until it makes a profit?
- Can I afford to do this?
- What is my plan 'B' if plan 'A' goes wrong?

Judge each situation differently; there are no blanket rules applying to all situations. Remember, whatever control measures are put in place to minimize risk, there is no armour against fate. Nothing is an absolute certainty; even if your business is doing well now, it may have to overcome difficulties in the future. To reduce the likelihood of business failure you have to learn to think and use your imagination, to solve current problems and those yet to come.

Scenario

A businessman needed a large loan for the purchase of a basement bar. If the business venture failed he would lose his house and end up in a rented flat, but he still decided to go ahead.

He managed to run the bar successfully for a while and it made a decent profit, until the anti-smoking legislation came in. He realized that he would lose a lot of custom because they had no beer garden or yard, so he sold the business immediately.

Within 18 months, the new owners became insolvent and the bar closed. If the businessman had not sold the bar when he did, he would have lost everything.

Stupid risks

Take calculated risks. That is quite different from being rash.

George S Patton, General, US Army, 1885–1945

The other type of risk is the stupid one. Relying on gut instincts can often be the deciding factor in judging a risk. **If a business deal doesn't feel right, your subconscious may be trying to tell you something; do not ignore it**.

However, relying on instinct alone isn't enough to be able to assess the likelihood of success or failure. Decision making needs to be informed by thinking through the consequences if things should go wrong. It is easy to make erroneous decisions and throw opportunity and money away. History shows us that many generations of businesspeople have made silly mistakes. Misjudgements are part of the process: Winston Churchill once said, 'Success is going from failure to failure with no loss of enthusiasm'. However, it is anticipated that lessons are learnt along the way.

Apply common sense to any situation. Here are a few points to remember:

- Do not rely too heavily on one customer or supplier. Never have too many eggs in one basket.
- Make sure any contracts received are fully understood, especially concerning the licensing of rights, such as software, brands, artwork, designs and patents. Read all the clauses, including opening words, and any other documents sent such as terms and conditions.
- Take out appropriate insurance cover before undertaking projects, especially those that carry personal liability.
- Avoid entering into ventures without considering a number of viewpoints and feedback from your team or advisers. A mono-viewpoint will ensure failure.

Closing thoughts

People who don't take risks generally make about two big mistakes a year.
People who do take risks generally make about two big mistakes a year.

Peter Drucker, business guru and author, 1909–2005

Enterprise and risk are joint partners in any venture. Any practical decisions must be based upon a firm premise in the form of research, planning and consultation. Relying only on your own perception is pure folly. To minimize failure you must have a balanced team of people you can talk to, or if you have a sole enterprise, have advisers that you can discuss business matters with. If you are surrounded by people who either all totally agree or disagree with you, then you need to take steps to recruit new people with differing views to cultivate an atmosphere of healthy debate.

Key Points

- Gain as much feedback as possible about a project and welcome constructive criticism. If you are a manager, cultivate a united team and be prepared to delegate.
- As well as learning from mistakes, undertaking risk assessment will help you make better decisions.
- Develop business disaster plans; for instance, could you still trade if you had a fire? What would happen to your business if you had an accident?
- Make a list of the likely problems you will face in the short and long term.
- What changes will you have to make to reduce the risk of problems or business failure?
- What do you hope to achieve from these changes? What do you need to improve and build on?

Enterprise skills booster

- What are your weaknesses? What are your strengths?
- What do you need to improve and build on?
  - a few business ideas you would like to develop if there was no risk of failure;
  - any barriers that are stopping you from moving forward;
  - situations you have been in before where you encountered barriers and managed to overcome them.
- What aspects need to change in your situation?
- If you changed these aspects, what difference would it make?
- Consider all the topics in Table 2.1 carefully, and undertake risks assessments on all relevant topics and any others you can think of.
- If you have a rapidly expanding or larger business, it may be worth investing in getting specialist help with risk assessments from professional advisers, such as business, finance or heath and safety experts.

3

Managing enterprising minds

Think.

IBM® slogan, invented by the company founder, Thomas J Watson,
1914–1993

There is an art to managing people, whether cultivating a small team or a much larger department. Encouraging an enterprising mindset among employees is especially important for a company that seeks to become a market leader in its sector.

Creative teamwork

A well-known UK investment bank prides itself on its participation in local community initiatives. As part of the bank's corporate social responsibility policy, it asks employees to take part in local cultural and environmental projects.

Activities range from creating gardens to public artworks with children and adults, often from deprived backgrounds. The bank's employees enjoy the experience of working in the community and improving local resources. The participants enjoy meeting new people, learning new skills and hearing about future career possibilities.

Members of your team may have connections with local community organizations that would value your help with ongoing projects. It is an opportunity for them to experience working together to complete a challenge in a creative environment.

Managing a team-enterprise

The Mind Map® can be applied to every aspect of life where improved learning and clearer thinking will enhance human performance.

Tony Buzan, psychologist and author, 1942–

Building an effective team is a challenging task, especially when managers have limited choices. It helps greatly if a team leader has the freedom to choose from a range of suitable candidates. As a manager, you have to organize a number of individuals who are dependent on each other for success. Whether the team is inherited or newly formed, it will be composed of people with a variety of qualities and skills.

When working with teams of people, especially those with mixed abilities, brainstorming and mind mapping on large pieces of paper can help them to gain an overview of the whole project. (To brainstorm is a means of generating ideas, whereas creating a mind map® is a method of organizing thoughts.) This is a more inspirational approach to exploring projects than explaining them with endless bullet points.

It is a proven fact that people process information in different ways. Communication is at its best when it brings together visual, verbal and interactive approaches. Creative activity such as group mapping does all three, and nurtures bonding. However, it is important that as team leader you organize these events carefully: that quieter members should be encouraged to contribute, and the more vocal should be reined in slightly. Some degree of 'air controlling' is important if the session is to go well. A good discussion will conclude with everyone feeling their contribution has been voiced and included in the map.

This approach is a good technique to foster creativity among team members – though implementing any plan still depends on having the right skills and approach. **It's not a magic panacea for all the company's problems, but it will highlight many unforeseen problems that could suddenly knock the project off course later on**.

Microsoft's multi-million dollar empire displays 'idea' boards around workspaces to keep creativity flowing. To keep its immense company's dominance in the software battlefield, innovation is the central hub of its strategy.

Tony and Barry Buzan have written excellent books about mind mapping. If you would like to read their most recent book and learn more about other approaches that may be of interest, see the recommendations in 'Further reading'.

Team-enterprise and risk management

Management that is destructively critical when mistakes are made, kills initiative. And it's essential that we have many people with initiative if we continue to grow.

William Mcknight, Chief Executive 3M™, 1887–1978

If we recall Table 2.1, in the second chapter, and consider ways to reduce the likelihood of failure, it is worth agreeing with your staff workable systems to reduce the chance of error, and not just to cope with unexpected events thrown up by destiny. With a united team approach, most problems can be resolved through making time in the week for 'double checking' measures.

Encouraging an enterprising mind...

It is important at the beginning of a project, when setting the schedule, that everyone shares in a united vision. This is where brainstorming and mind mapping play their role, activities that are designed to actively engage and empower team members.

It is vital that concerns about taking risks do not become a barrier to staff developing an enterprising outlook. The manager has to nurture the team's creativity by encouraging them to share responsibility for any risky decisions. Eliminating blame culture will assist in generating a positive climate for boldness.

Barriers to risk taking

The only man who never makes a mistake is the man who never does anything.

Theodore Roosevelt, US President and statesman, 1858–1919

One of the great obstacles to stimulating enterprising attitudes among staff, as mentioned in the previous chapter, is the fear of making mistakes, being held accountable for failure, or at best being made a fool of. Any good manager should ask for 'group ownership' by the team of any exciting ideas suggested. In business, things do go wrong occasionally, and holding individuals to blame will not help. All it will do is stop your team from making future contributions.

It may require patience and some investment of time to cultivate an enterprising outlook among your team. To promote creative thinking and reduce the risk of misfortune, nurture a culture in which the whole group takes responsibility. In the advertising world, companies work using this kind of approach. Without it, that next innovation will just not happen. Generating a positive atmosphere and a happy environment are fundamental factors in team building.

Minimizing the risk of failure

Boldness has genius, power and magic in it.

Johann Wolfgang von Goethe, poet and novelist, 1749–1832

It is important that managers encourage innovation within their team. However, it is equally pertinent that managers foresee what might go wrong, and stop their team doing things that would lead to disaster. This is why making time to check for mistakes is vital.

It is worth creating workable systems that reduce the possibility of problems occurring in the first place. Reduce the possibility of failure by spreading risk across a team (this approach also improves team dynamics). For instance, when chairing meetings it is important to let the group decide the agenda together. Involving the team in making the agenda will empower each individual member. Managing meetings in an intrapreneurial fashion reduces the likelihood of people quitting projects or their jobs.

Each individual will have different interests and viewpoints of a project. It is advisable that everyone is allotted a time slot to discuss their particular concerns. Putting such activity into 'Any other business', at the end of long meetings, will apply pressure on those who have had to wait to the end, when most people wish to leave, to express their viewpoint. Contributors who wait a long time to be heard and then are not given appropriate consideration will, over time, become disgruntled. Restlessness and the perception of not being listened to is a recipe for disaster. The last thing any manager wants is good people disengaging from a project, and walking out at possibly a crucial stage.

Dealing with difficult people

If at the start of a project it becomes evident that a team member has a completely different view at odds with the group, then there are several ways of dealing with opposing ideas. First, objectors may have valid points; they may have noticed difficulties which others haven't. Second, it can help to have such a person in a team: it will assist everyone to think through their ideas carefully, as they know they will be analysed and subject to criticism. Walt Disney always said it was a good idea to keep critics within the organization. However, he frequently did lose his patience and sacked dissenters, though he always reinstated them after a cooling-off period. Arguments become stronger if they survive nit-picking.

If objectors are at total loggerheads with the rest of the team, they can just end up being an utter nuisance and draining everyone's energies. There are many tactics for dealing with difficult people, such as asking them at the beginning of meetings 'to prepare a few words' to say on a particular issue at the end of the meeting. This may keep them quiet as they think through their thoughts, while the rest of the day's business is agreed. Another approach is to send them off to undertake research to back up their argument. Alternatively, if they are just being difficult and their ideas cannot be substantiated, then perhaps it is best if they can be persuaded to join another team or be given a different role in the project. It is sometimes better to let a team member go at the start of a project then at any other time.

Sharing tasks to reduce the risk of failure

Another aspect of managing risk is the importance of building in safety mechanisms. When agreeing which team members undertake certain tasks, there may be certain activities that carry a heavier burden than others. If you consider the task of marketing for a product launch or exhibition, it is always better to have a few people sharing the work. If only one team member has the plan, all the copy, plus media contact deals, and for some reason that person falls ill as important deadlines approach, then press packs or even admission tickets will not arrive in good time, with disastrous consequences. Therefore, it is vital that a few people share the responsibility for these tasks.

Closing thoughts

Good management is the art of making problems so interesting and their solutions so constructive that everyone wants to get to work and deal with them.

Paul Hawken, entrepreneur and author, 1946–

As well as creativity, enterprising managers must acquire a range of interpersonal skills, an almost perceptive intelligence, an inquiring mind and the foresight to plan activities over a long period of time. This quote by the environmental entrepreneur Paul Hawken sums up my thoughts about intrapreneurial management perfectly. If your team are fully engaged in the process, the chances of mistakes being made will be significantly diminished.

Key points

- Think about each of your team member's attributes, skills, strengths and weaknesses. What roles would suit them? Are current team members suited to their current responsibilities?
- Be prepared to experiment with different ways of organizing meetings, activities and projects.
- How will you monitor projects for mistakes and errors? What new systems would you like to try for a few months and by what means can you assess any improvements made?
- Trust is a key component in team building. How can you check that team members are happy with their workload, environment, career prospects, etc.
- If employees are unhappy then it is likely they will lose motivation or even leave. Try to find solutions to minor irritations now, rather then wait until they build up to more serious problems.

- Invest in seeking advice from creative consultants or team-building facilitators about new ways to stimulate creativity and improve team dynamics.

Enterprise skills booster

- Set up a feedback box where staff can post suggestions, ideas or raise concerns.
- Create an ideas board; this can be in the form of a physical board where team members can stick up cards or Post-it notes. Alternatively leave your mind map® up on the wall with extra sheets of paper, so contributors can add more observations or radiant thoughts. Try to avoid having everything as digital display only; this can actually make the brainstorming and mind mapping processes less spontaneous, unless you have expensive interactive software and display equipment.
- What other activities would help your team to bond in creative ways?
- Experiment if budgets and time will allow, with different creative activities, such as lunchtime music sessions using small drums and percussion instruments. This is an easy activity to organize and anyone can take part. Quiz nights, sports activities, trips to the theatre are all popular ways to raise morale and engage staff in different contexts.
- Does your firm have a corporate social responsibility policy? If not why not?
- Engaging with the community is not just about good PR. There are many ways your team could help local charities indirectly, by gaining sponsorship for fun runs, or other unusual methods of raising cash such as breaking world records.

4

How to focus

At the age of six I wanted to be a cook. At seven I wanted to be Napoleon. My ambition has been growing ever since.

Salvador Dali, artist, 1904–1989

Discovering which direction in life to explore can be an unpredictable endeavour. For instance, most of us would agree that ambitions of early childhood radically change as adulthood approaches. The idea of setting up a business as a realistic career option may not have occurred to people until after their school years have ended. However, it is equally relevant that many famous entrepreneurs embarked upon remarkable initiatives while teenagers. Many do not gain academic qualifications, opting to gain employment or hatch their own fledging enterprises.

One reason so few of us achieve what we truly want is that we never direct our focus; we never concentrate our power. Most people dabble their way through life, never deciding to master anything in particular.

Anthony Robbins, author and motivational speaker, 1960–

Creating focus can take some people decades to achieve. **One barrier to making progress is attempting far too many activities at a time, and never really making much headway with any of them.** Another is facing too many distractions; examples include the over-committed parent forced to juggle work and childcare responsibilities, or simply those with an inquisitive nature who just take on too many commitments. It is easy to become distracted by the television, internet or leisure software. The skill is to try to avoid losing valuable time and cluttering the mind with rubbish.

Environment

Never again clutter your days and nights with so many menial things that you have no time to accept a real challenge when it comes along.

Og Mandino, American essayist and psychologist, 1923–1996

It is easy 'to busy' oneself. Are you preoccupied with making intelligent strides towards achieving progress or just expending energy with no firm purpose?

Applying oneself to a selective course of action can be difficult when passions are mixed up with ambition. It is true to say that businessmen and women are in love with their work, hopefully not just because they are earning money, but because it excites and interests them. Many successful business leaders in their early lives explored different areas of trade before putting all their energies and resources into one venture. After this had grown into a profitable enterprise, some diversified while others sold their business to generate capital to invest in new companies.

Whatever route they took, they all shared an ability to make rational judgements about their business proposals, and to separate emotions from the equation. Take the showbiz impresario Simon Cowell, who has initiated talent contests around the world. Whenever he has to cast a difficult deciding vote between two contestants, he asks himself, shall I listen to my heart or my head? A man who has made hundreds of millions of pounds will always opt for the latter.

How do you gain focus?

One of the keys to thinking big is total focus. I think of it almost as a controlled neurosis, which is a quality I've noticed in many highly successful entrepreneurs.

Donald Trump, successful entrepreneur, 1946–

First, consider your physical environment. It is commonplace to find computers and televisions in bedrooms and rest areas. Many offices are now open plan, with resulting background chatter and likelihood of disturbance. Where can you escape to get some peace?

Is it possible to create a place where you can start to think? Is it really relaxing to simultaneously send e-mails, watch TV and gobble snacks? Is this quiet contemplation or just a chaotic environment? To create space either at home, work or another location is important; this is where focus can begin.

Change your environment

Three rules of work:
Out of clutter find simplicity.
From discord find harmony.
In the middle of difficulty lies opportunity.

Albert Einstein, theoretical physicist, 1879–1955

Your next step is to make adjustments to your environment, whether at home or in the office, or both! What can be thrown away or perhaps stored elsewhere? Make time to get rid of clutter and organize posses-sions so everything has its place. Many people suffer from a difficulty of throwing things away. It takes time to recover from being a hoarder. Asking a friend or colleague to assist in throwing junk away can be helpful – encouragement can make the whole process less daunting. Set a target of perhaps a third of all junk, or perhaps all the piles and boxes of stuff in one particular room.

It is possible to apply enterprising attitudes to this first step. There may be goods that can be auctioned off, sold to neighbours at car boot or garage sales. Never underestimate what other people are willing to buy. The founder of eBay™, Pierre Omidyar, said his first sale was a broken laser pointer, which sold for US $14.83. Once all the clutter has gone, you can make room for the future.

Looking ahead

Map out your future, but do it in pencil.

Jon Bon Jovi, musician and singer, 1962–

After the purge, it is time to apply a similar process to your own life. In the newly made space, place an A1 year planner on the wall for the year ahead. If possible, invest in a blank one to make up for the following year. If it is a big project or idea, it is likely that a visual map of the next 12–24 months is desirable. Once it is up there, it will appear like a void. Some people at first find it disconcerting to see time in this format.

When planning a business and preparing to achieve goals, plot them out on the planner. It is impossible to plan on a weekly or monthly basis, as many aspects of business such as project management or planning a marketing campaign require a schedule over many months or years in advance. Many businesses treat their wall planners as ornamental features. Don't just absentmindedly put the special pen and coloured stickers in a drawer; make use of them. Turn the planner into a visual tool by colour-coding activities.

Barriers to focus

One of the symptoms of an approaching nervous breakdown is the belief that one's work is terribly important.

Bertrand Russell, author and philosopher, 1872–1970

In Chapter 8 we will be exploring how to manage time wisely. However, to achieve concentration, more analysis of current lifestyles is required. To progress in business requires a total commitment to a particular project. I recall a student who once said in an enterprise seminar that he had trouble completing tasks before more were asked of him. Business guru Stephen Covey articulates in his books many useful theories of how to organize activities in a systematic format. I concur with all that Covey says. When working alone, there is only one sequence available: as soon as there is a team, progress can be made on many fronts. One can argue that a multi-tasking individual can achieve much, though tasks still have to be completed in a methodical manner.

Returning to the underlying problem of the student, are there simply too many demands on his time? Should he simply turn down requests to do things, or not undertake so many?

There will always be periods in the week or month where we may over-work to achieve a target. However, if we are constantly under pressure, this eventually will lead to stress, with at least one consequence being poor decision making. It can take people time to realize that their working day is ever lengthening, with increasingly early starts, late clocking off, then working through weekends. Overwork combined with lack of sleep is another factor that does impair ability to function in many areas. Tiredness significantly affects concentration.

This subject interlinks with developing a positive mindset, planning and legal issues. All of these topics require energy and being alert. If you are tired, it's probable you will make a mistake, which could have all kinds of consequences. Therefore, take stock of your life, cut down on fruitless distractions, and most of all get a good night's sleep.

Another factor that hinders focus is becoming dehydrated. Research indi-cates that 2 per cent body dehydration leads to a 20 per cent decrease in concentration. Not getting enough holiday time can contribute to poor performances. Becoming run-down over time will lead to exhaustion. A change of environment is good, not only to recharge batteries, but to gain a fresh perspective.

Factors that force focus

It is worth considering that a new direction can be triggered by other factors such as life-changing circumstances. If we recall preparing for examinations either as children or as adults, I am sure we can all remember sitting alone with index cards, essays and assignments, trying urgently to absorb facts into our memories. Staying indoors, as if living under a curfew, trying to remember huge swathes of information; all this may be very much at odds with our usual behaviour. Yet, think back; you did stay in for many weeks and, yes, finally passed those exams.

Imagine waking up one morning and then arriving at work to be told by the boss that the company is in financial difficulty and is letting staff go. Losing your job or being made redundant can result in mental chaos for a short time. Then suddenly the daily driving force is searching for a new position. Equally, it could be an opportunity to explore that business idea you have long been thinking about. Paul Arden, the great art director, comments in his books (see 'Further reading') that getting the sack can be the making of people. Sometimes, being pushed into a new direction can be a good thing.

It is amazing what is achievable when you are up against it. Any sudden strange event can make people re-evaluate what is important to them. Priorities alter when there is a dramatic change in the status quo, forcing the mind to refocus.

Vision

You cannot depend on your judgments when your imagination is out of focus.

Mark Twain, humorist and writer, 1835–1910

To achieve any goal in life requires ambition and the desire to fulfil a dream. Others may view it as an unrealistic aspiration. Listen to constructive feedback, but don't be put off by the doubtful. Whatever the big picture, making little achievable steps towards it ensures progress. Steps are best if they become strides towards realizing vision. Whether working alone or with others, it is vital to formulate a destination to which the journey will lead.

The greatest danger for us all is not that we aim too high and we miss it, but that it is too low and we reach it.

Michelangelo, artist, 1475–1564

There are many reasons why having a substantial idea is essential. Visualization, among other benefits, is vital to motivate and enthuse others. Mohammed Ali famously would visualize contests in his mind, as if watching a movie, working out in which round he would knock out his opponent. His predictions frequently were realized. He combined self-belief with a mental focus that channelled his energies.

Making it work

To realize a large undertaking demands a strategy. An essential element is to gather enthusiastic supporters who will help make a theoretical plan reality. Big ideas are achieved by assembling a cohort of experts who will be able to give advice, and even assist in getting the venture off the ground.

All the skills and risks discussed so far have to be readily applied. The proposition has to be tested, to calculate whether it is worth pursuing. It is no good putting energies into something, however passionate you feel, if for example the proposal already exists as a patent, or is infeasible due to current restrictive regulation.

To make it happen, apart from fastidious preparation, and sometimes a great deal of money, there are other less predictable factors in play such as luck and opportunity; they make it truly possible for wishes to be fulfilled. There are vast numbers of UK patent applications, over 90 per cent of which never reach the marketplace as saleable products. It is likely that so many fail due to inventors making avoidable mistakes, lacking a strategy and failing to master enterprise skills.

I recall a photograph published in a magazine that I saw as a teenager of a technician standing with a yoke of wires round his neck and metal boxes in either hand. It captured the first working prototype of a 'portable' computer. My friends and I thought to conceive of such a thing was totally ridiculous. Why on earth would people wish to carry computers around with them?

At the time of writing, Richard Branson is beginning to trial his VSS Voyager. I wonder, when he started out all those years ago, when entirely reliant on a coin-operated public phone box to run his business, if he ever imagined that before the end of the century he would be selling tickets for his own pioneering commercial spaceflights. The Virgin founder, as in previous expeditions, may indeed co-pilot Voyager's maiden flight. If you are reading this book while on board, then it is evident that – however outlandish some notions may be – anything is possible.

Be willing to make a serious effort

What is the secret of your success?
Call me at my office any Friday night at 10 o'clock and I'll tell you.

Professor Randy Pausch, professor of computer science, 1960–2008

Business planning, finance and effective networking are three ingredients that will make the achievement of any original idea more likely (though bear in mind the relevance of focus). I recall working as an adviser, and observing some clients hurriedly writing their business plans while waiting in reception for their appointments. I used to wonder what an earth was going on in their minds. Could it be that they wish to set up a business, and their focus is such that the fundamental task of writing the plan is the very last priority? Some clients wished to set up magazines and other enormous initiatives that might require years of commitment and hundreds of thousands of pounds. Yet here they were a few minutes before a meeting, scribbling away.

I also remember a business course, when at the beginning the students were advised to visit a business start-up expo. Not one of the students found the time to go. These two examples demonstrate that it is only a minority of the populace who are truly driven and achieve great things.

Time has to be made for researching, planning and application. Many clients and students suddenly make great strides once they have learnt some skills, cut down on trying to pursue too many ideas at once and achieved focus.

Goals

Your vision of where or who you want to be is the greatest asset you have.
Without having a goal it's difficult to score.

Paul Arden, art director, 1940–2008

Goals are important milestones in the journey. They should be specific, measured, achievable, realistic, targeted and timed. Make sure that the targets for the next 12 months are realistic. Even if you fail to achieve them, it is likely some degree of progress towards them will be made. If after a few weeks from starting a venture little is achieved, then it is important to analyse why this is.

- Is it because you have been over-ambitious?
- Insufficient resources available?
- Lack of funds?
- Proposals rejected?
- Trying to do too many things?

Any form of creative or experimental enterprise can take a lot longer to establish than is commonly supposed. This can easily derail interest in a project with the result that pioneers or team members lose heart. Sometimes ideas are simply unworkable, so this is where long-term flexible goals are vital. Future objectives can be for between 3 and 10 years ahead. They should envisage a range of outcomes in order to maintain other options in the event of initial failure. It is essential not to give up when things go wrong. Consider going in a different direction if the first is not a success.

Many successful people began in different fields from those in which they achieved their fortune. Simon Woodroffe, entrepreneur and founder of Yo! Sushi®, funded his initiative in his early 40s from the proceeds of a divorce settlement. Originally, he had a career in the music industry. Geoffrey Palmer, a well-known British actor, was previously in the army and took up the stage at the age of 40. In fact, he did not get his first TV break until he was 50. Oprah Winfrey started out as a reporter, became a TV talk show host and is now a television network owner. John Lennon was among many other musicians who spent their formative years studying at art college. Part of being entrepreneurial is being flexible to change and circumstance.

Changing gear

Plan your work for today, and every day, then work your plan.

Margaret Thatcher, British Prime Minister and stateswoman, 1925–

If you are advancing nicely, with ticks against completed tasks on 'to do lists', then the original project plan was correctly determined. It now may be the right time to crank up the pressure slightly and drive further forward.

Bite off more than you can chew, then chew it.

Ella D Williams, CEO Aegir Systems, 1940–

There is a lot to be said for taking on more than you think is achievable. I meet many fledgling business owners who have turned down sudden orders or work because they didn't believe they could deliver. More entrepreneurial clients recount similar tales of the unexpected shortly after they started trading, as they were sitting alone in a studio or office. The phone unexpectedly rang and a client asked if they could fulfil a £35,000 order in the next three months. All they remember is instinctively saying 'yes' confidently, even through they had no staff and few resources, then after the call has ended, experiencing an outburst of complete panic.

Progress and growth will never be achieved if you're not willing to put effort in and take a few risks. Events good, bad or surprising will occur during your business life. It is how one reacts and manages such situations that matters most.

Determination

Genius is 1 per cent inspiration and 99 per cent perspiration.

Thomas Alva Edison, inventor, 1847–1931

Determination is a quality that you may naturally possess. It is essential in realizing any ambitious ideas. Equally, perseverance is a desirable attribute to improve economic circumstances and escape poverty. Determination to succeed in an endeavour can require you to forego a social life, luxuries and sometimes sleep. Entrepreneurs have to become resilient to rejection and view failure as a learning curve. Toughness may not yet be a key characteristic of your personality, though after experiencing the harsher side of business life, one becomes more resilient in nature. It is likely that a great amount of hard work will have to be undertaken so major goals can be accomplished. So be prepared to adopt the pursuit skills of a bloodhound, and remember the words of Bill Clinton (a political survivor if ever there was one): 'The main thing is never quit, never quit, never quit.'

Achieving team goals

The achievement of one goal should be the starting point of another.

Alexander Graham Bell, inventor, 1847–1922

We all know the secret of management is delegation. Mind maps® can be an invisible tool to allocate duties to team members. This will temporarily relieve you of this often irksome responsibility.

When brainstorming with colleagues, there will be a number of identifiable ideas and tasks. These will form the action plan to make objectives achievable. Make connections between them, in the form of themes. For instance, the mind map® can be used as a tool to order random scribbles. Topical suggestions can be entered in circles with titles such as 'legal', 'communication', 'budget', 'planning' and 'marketing'. Then from this rough outline, you can make a more coherent version.

During the exercise, you could ask people which areas of the project they would like to work on. It is possible that some employees always undertake the same activities. Be prepared to move the furniture around occasionally, and encourage team members to try different tasks. This will stop them becoming bored with stale routines. Team members will be pleased and more enthusiastic about their work as they have decided what to do for themselves, without having to be 'told' what to do.

In managing a team it is good to motivate staff by rewards. Bonuses are always well received; a party or treating everyone to lunch are other options. It is advantageous to stimulate your team's commitment to targets. A common error is setting numerous impossible goals for your team and yourself as well!

Many employees, if faced with jumping through ever-increasing numbers of hoops, will become jaded and cynical over time. If little relation between pay and effort is perceived, team members will become demotivated. Applying penalties – the less carrot more beating with stick approach – will upset people and lead to resignations. As we will discuss later, 'goodwill' is an intangible asset. Contented staff will work hard. To keep the workforce happy and loyal, the team leader must build respect and trust. When goodwill is lost, only slow progress towards goals will be made.

Closing thoughts

A goal is a dream with a dateline.

Napoleon Hill, author, 1883–1970

Business owners or managers often have to look beyond what they think is achievable. When business objectives are met with team celebrations, this will encourage the team to put more effort into future ambitions.
When failing to achieve all targets, one has to be philosophical. It doesn't matter if all that was hoped for was not won. If all the stops have been pulled out, and the majority were completed more or less on time, then sometimes that is the best that can be hoped for. Delays, budget problems and mistakes can substantially knock any project off course. Sustaining big ideas is difficult. If achieving greatness was easy, then we would all have amassed personal fortunes!

Key points

- Clear out new space, rid your desk of old documents.

- Examine your computer; can your files be slimmed down or reorganized?

- Think about activities that will improve focus such as reading, meditating, walking, playing chess, listening to music or learning to play an instrument. Try one of these activities for 10 minutes every morning without interruption. Then every week increase the exercise by 10 minutes, until you build up to an hour.

- Cut down on excessive commitments and any distractions that fragment your time.

- Decide what you would like to achieve in the next 10 years. Do you still wish to live at your present address? Would you be happy in a decade's time living on a similar amount of salary or profit? If the answer is 'no' to either of these questions, how will you change the situation?

- Brainstorm and make a mind map® capturing ideas, future vision and goals.

Enterprise skills booster

- If you are a manager, what incentives could keep your team motivated? Ask your team individually what they would like: cash bonus, a mini-break, music or book vouchers, gym membership, a change in the dress code, lunch vouchers, support with childcare, flexible working or other incentives.

- If you are starting a business, think about all your business ideas, write each of them down on Post-it notes and stick them on the wall.
    - Now just pick one, for the moment, to pursue further.
    - What three steps can you take in the next 10 days to progress towards your first goal?

- Imagine the year is 2020 and you are throwing a party to celebrate a major achievement. What have you accomplished?

- In the future, what would you like to be remembered for?

You wake up one morning to find £300,000 or US $600,000 in your lap. A note is attached to it, explaining you can invest it in any business idea apart from the stock or property markets. What would you do with this much money?

This exercise is to help you in generating a vision for a business, which could be a 5- or 10-year goal. The offer of a large sum of money is to help you visualize long-term goals.

The next day you wake up to find another note in your lap. It advises you that it is wise to gain expert help to get your idea going. It then says:

Who would you like to talk to?
Some ideas are included in the matrix below (Table 4.1). Please ring five sources of advice.
OK, the promise of money and experts wasn't true.

However, if you have an original idea then get help with writing a business plan. With a confident pitch, it is more likely you will get the money from a bank or private investor to make your dream a reality.

Table 4.1 Advisers and consultants

Business adviser	Financial adviser	Investor	Accountant
Solicitor	Mentor	Coach	Creative thinker
Image and presentation expert	Public relations consultant	Branding consultant	Marketing consultant
Entrepreneur	Designer	Inventor	Photographer
Chartered surveyor	Architect	Builder	Civil engineer

5

The importance of networking

Man cannot discover new oceans unless he has the courage to lose sight of the shore.

André Gide, novelist and poet, 1869–1951

To start and succeed in business involves the effort of going out and meeting new people. It can even require willingness to leave your hometown or country to achieve success. Many entrepreneurs, and managers employed by global firms, commonly go on fact-finding missions or periodically work abroad.

Remember the poetic description from 1934 of enterprise as an 'undertaking' that requires 'courage' and the 'readiness to engage'. It is vital that you develop these qualities as being willing to build rapport, sometimes with complete strangers, is how opportunities are discovered. The mind map®, Figure 3.1, shows how networking relates to accomplishing goals. It is through the 'readiness to engage' with new people that you will develop a business vision. Planning requires the participation of other businessmen and women you have still yet to meet.

What is networking?

> ## Networking
>
> Making use of meetings with other people involved in the same kind of work, in order to share information and help each other.
>
> *Longman Business Dictionary, 2000*

In the 1980s networking had a bad press, and was viewed as a shallow and egocentric activity. We now live in more enlightened times when business, especially in the UK, is better understood than it used to be.

The world is beginning to change. Networking can now be conducted in numerous ways, both on and offline. This mirrors a less formal atmosphere in the commercial domain. For example, there are many chief executives who are rarely seen in public dressed in a formal suit and tie, Richard Branson, Bill Gates and Richard Reed for example. (Though traditionalists such as the billionaire entrepreneur Peter Jones will beg to differ.) When Wayne Hemmingway, the British designer, joined the Institute of Directors, the dress code for members required the wearing of a pinstriped suit and tie. Wayne turned up dressed in a woman's pinstriped business jacket and skirt. This did cause the raising of eyebrows. The stunt also triggered a debate about how the new generation of entrepreneurs wish to conduct their business.

Casual attire represents a shift in the image of business. It symbolizes modern inclusive interaction. Wearing the uniform of yesteryear is still popular in many corporate sectors, though the changing forms of business structure (ie more micro-enterprises than large firms) mean that many business people take a more relaxed view of how businesses can be run. Many home workers will testify how pyjamas make perfect daywear! Within this evolving environment, networking has also had a makeover, with a new message: it is a way to engage with others for mutual advantage.

Why network?

If you wait for opportunities to occur, you will be one of the crowd.

Edward De Bono, creative thinking guru, 1933–

As a growth strategy, meeting other enterprising individuals will help your business prosper. Networking is an inexpensive way of marketing a business, and it assists in raising the profile of brands, products and services. To find out more about networking opportunities, subscribe to e-mail news loops from local business clubs, regional support agencies or professional/trade bodies. The only expenses will be annual subscriptions to business associations or buying tickets for networking events, expos or conferences. What it does involve in terms of cost is that of time and energy.

Napoleon Hill in *Master Key to Riches* (2007) outlines the importance of forming 'master mind alliances' for 'business, professional and economic advancement'. As you can see in Figure 5.1, it is impossible to start a venture with no contacts. Business friends are crucial, not only as potential sources of opportunities but to help in times of crisis. Friends with whom you go to the pub on a Friday night are just as important as business friends. However, favours can be asked from the latter, such as advice, assistance or resources. Networking is a two-way activity, as the *Longman Dictionary* puts it, to 'help each other'. It is not just about taking, but also giving. The worst kind of networking is when it is one sided. Avoid draining others for information, and offering little in return.

Being in the know

Books, magazines and web articles can be anywhere from two minutes to years old. It's sometimes difficult to tell how old 'recent' published research data actually is, so make sure you check how up to date it is before basing business decisions on it. Consumer demands, trends, economies, governments and laws are always in flux. **Networking, meeting with peers or more established business owners, can give a valuable insight into what is currently happening in the marketplace**. How can you make accurate decisions without up-to-date industry knowledge?

Don't wait for some kind of 'discovery' moment in life. No one is going to come along with all the answers. Andrew Carnegie, the American steel magnate, wrote at great length about this (Hill, 2007). He thought too many people believed 'in luck or miracles' that they hope will favour them. It is simply unrealistic just to rely on chance. You have to be

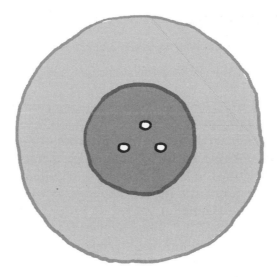

Figure 5.1 You can't start a business in isolation

bold, and act by targeting those who can help through establishing new networks.

It can be difficult to predict what kind of networking events, whether formal or informal, will be advantageous. The route to success can be invisible – it may not be obvious who needs to be targeted and why. You may not be clear about what you want to achieve. This is why setting goals is fundamental when venturing out in the world.

The strategy you set out for yourself needs both systematic and provisional elements. For example, if the business needs an input of specialized services to ensure targets are reached in 12 months' time, then it is futile to wait until the last minute to start looking for them. It may take longer than first anticipated to find the right people or suppliers, and when you eventually wish to place an order or make a booking the supplier might be unable to provide services at short notice. If experts are hired in the short term, then it is more likely long-term targets will be accomplished by the end of the year.

It is important to allow for some experimental networking, away from a rigid plan. Make time, to speak with those you may not think relevant to the predetermined plan. That chance encounter near the espresso machine may yield surprising results.

Spotting opportunities

Small opportunities are often the beginning of great enterprises.

Demosthenes, Athenian statesman, 384 or (383) BC–322 BC

In busy towns and cities there are possibilities everywhere. With flexible employment and business laws, people can work or set up a business anywhere. With the expansion of the internet, even those living in remote villages are able to earn a living by e-trading from home. Developing connections in the real and virtual world increases everyone's options. The more clients you are able to make aware of your products and services, the better.

Don't be downhearted about attracting only small commissions or projects initially. You cannot be sure how these may blossom into larger openings. One hundred per cent of business is based upon trust. Trust in the early stages of any relationship is cultivated in small ways, such as turning up on time, doing a good job and meeting deadlines. Once rapport between yourself and the fledgling client grows, substantial opportunities can follow.

The reluctant networker

A builder, who did not see the point of networking, was constantly urged by his girlfriend to attend networking events organized by a local enterprise agency. Eventually he decided to go, spurred on by the fact that his order book was empty.

When he arrived at the event he was disappointed to find only a handful of people had turned up. He decided to leave, but before he had time to put his coat back on a property developer approached him. There was an instant rapport between them which resulted in the builder gaining a regular client. He continued to offer the builder contracts for the next 10 years.

Contacts can be found in the most unpromising of circumstances. This one chance meeting turned into a profitable arrangement for both parties.

Social networks

It is not what you know, but who you know.

Paul Arden, art director and author, 1940–2008

How do you create a networking database or meet new people? Social networks can be developed anywhere from childhood companions to new friends at evening classes. If you are an individual, start to record contact details of friends, fellow students or colleagues; if a manager, have a look at the firm's database (check when it was last updated, as it may not be fit for current purposes).

Social networks

There has been a huge explosion in online social networking, blogs and local networking groups. Facebook, Linkedin®, myspace™, YouTube, Saga, among many such web services, are new ways of meeting people from around the world with similar ambitions to yours by uploading your profile and connecting with them. If you decide to make use of social networks, try to focus on quality rather than quantity. Be selective about where you showcase, as keeping profiles up to date and responding to messages takes time. Equally, there is a danger that particular showcasing or networking websites won't attract real opportunities, and engaging with them is simply a waste of time.

A selection of popular networking websites:
www.facebook.com
www.linkedin.com
www.myspace.com
www.bebo.com
www.wayn.com
www.sagazone.co.uk
www.friendsreunited.co.uk
www.ecademy.com
www.xing.com
www.madspace.co.uk

Professional associations

Next, list professional and other bodies in your field of activity. There are many business clubs and sector-specific associations that offer useful services, from networking events to the provision of industrial information. It is advisable to join such organizations. It may be a useful experience to sign up for a year or so before moving on. Equally, one may discover that the support they offer is invaluable, and embark on lifelong membership.

Professional bodies are an essential source of relevant news and opportunities. Many membership organizations offer subscribers an online directory or showcasing space on their websites, notice boards, chat rooms and blogging facilities. It's worth remembering that many customers check with professional bodies first before hiring suppliers, to confirm their credentials.

Special interest groups

Special interest groups and periodicals are of central importance in promoting a business at a minimal cost. There are hundreds of societies and publications serving tens of thousands of subscribers. Contributors range from readers who are specific collectors to those with other interests such as sports, science, business, management, IT, marketing, art and design, horticulture, lifestyle, heritage and ecology. Small or larger circulation magazines are usually open to receiving interesting features or articles. Many associations, such as The Royal Society for the Protection of Birds, RSPB, send out catalogues to their members, featuring calendars, tableware and textiles, decorated with bird-related illustrations or photographs.

Perhaps your products or services have nothing to do with special interest groups. Is it possible to make them so? Would more customers be attracted to a product if it was modified to appeal to them? Business relationships formed with popular causes can attract new customers through publicizing donations. In the UK, the RSPB is very popular; it has over a million members, more than all the UK political parties put together. Such associations will not be of use to all. However, if there is a chance they could be, further research may prove fruitful.

Local groups and community organizations

Groups that meet regularly or host annual events may be interested in inviting you to speak or hire a stand at a show. A businesswoman I once knew made her first sales from giving a talk and demonstration at a local women's circle. She then went on to repeat the experience with other female-based clubs and succeeded in forming an initial client base.

Expos and events

Visiting conferences and expos is not simply about undertaking market research but another approach to building contacts. If a stand-holder is momentarily unoccupied, seize the moment to make an introduction and find out about their business. Always remember, they are under pressure to talk to customers, so be brief, and follow up with further enquiries later by phoning or making the effort to visit. Do avoid overly relying on e-mail; everyone these days is spammed out. You can't build relations with e-mails; it is simply not the same as spontaneous interaction.

Calling in...

Going out of your way to call upon past or current customers is another means of developing a relationship. Busy entrepreneurs and managers may argue there isn't enough time in the week to make such visits! Ask yourself this question: what proportion of profit is generated from repeat orders? Is it a static percentage or is it slowly increasing? The likely answer is that to some degree the business relies upon a number of regular clients. Going to see them is not just about generating more sales; it is also about checking that they are content with services, and a chance to gain valuable feedback about earlier transactions.

It is characteristic of many people that they don't complain, and would rather not tell you what's wrong, preferring to go quietly off and find new suppliers. This is why making the effort to entertain or just dropping in for a cup of tea can be a chance to discover if there is any lurking dissatisfaction. It is better to rectify any problems during a friendly chat, rather than lose a customer. Every business owner knows it is far easier to make repeat sales to existing customers than acquire a new one.

Business and trade associations

Business clubs provide socials in the form of lunches or business breakfasts; these are usually local affairs. Larger associations and trade bodies host annual conferences attracting national and international delegates. It is useful to attend these events to gain an overview of new business developments. They can be excellent for profile raising, especially if you are asked to make a presentation, or for large firms to contribute through sponsoring the event.

The perils of alcohol

But I'm not so think as you drunk I am.

Sir John Collins Squire, poet and writer, 1884–1958

Other contacts can be generated by meeting friends through extended networks. It is prudent to bear in mind that any interaction in pubs or clubs serving alcohol can create problems. First, members of some faith groups do not wish to drink alcohol, thus making it difficult to participate fully in particular activities. Second, certain types of club, such as lap dancing venues, can make female members of a group uncomfortable. Third, under the influence of drink disastrous blunders can be made, with lasting consequences for your reputation.

Respect in business or management roles takes time to build. The old axiom 'avoid mixing business and pleasure' is worth considering. If you do decide to blend enterprise with entertainment, avoid inebriation and becoming a bore. People who talk too much about money or work while others are expecting to relax and enjoy themselves can be off-putting.

Alcohol is usually provided at other business events. When attending networking events avoid bringing along friends who suffer from drink problems; it could be a disastrous move. See such friends socially, but do not involve them in business matters.

When visiting events, make sure that you have eaten, as drinking, especially champagne on an empty stomach, can have unpredictable consequences. I have witnessed quite placid people become overly boisterous under the influence of drink. Try to moderate any intake; it is not beneficial to be recollected by potential business contacts as a 'drunk'.

Beyond the comfort zone

The threads of connections run everywhere and to unexpected places.

Susan Griffin, essayist and screenwriter, 1943–

Being strategic

Moving beyond the circle of friends, family and associates can take some time. To create a pool of contacts means identifying specific individuals, then undertaking research about them, before deciding who to approach. It is important to decide why you desire to court the attention of particular people or business owners. Is it because their help is required? Perhaps you hope that they will become excellent customers or suppliers. Becoming familiar with the background of key players in your sector is vital. When meeting them, being knowledgeable about their achievements will assist the development of mutual admiration.

Growing contacts

Creativity and growth depend on considering new ideas and bringing talented individuals into your circle or team.

Stepping out of familiar environments can be a daunting prospect. Figure 5.2 demonstrates how it is possible to make contact with people far outside your comfort zone. Susan Griffin's quote sums up Stanley Milgram's pioneering research, commonly referred to as the 'six degrees of separation' theory. Recent investigations into social networks by other psychologists, such as Richard Wiseman (2004a and b), suggest that the number of separating links is decreasing. This is due in part to present-day global communication systems, which 50 years ago could best be described as basic.

Note to professional managers

When exploring life outside the inner sphere, it is very helpful to find business contacts or other colleagues who are willing to introduce or recommend your services to others. Word of mouth, as mentioned before, is the best form of free advertising. However, it is rare for people to do this in the context of making an introduction. Your contemporaries may also be your competitors, and will not wish to help if it results in diminishing their own prospects. Always be alert to professional jealously; it takes many forms. Those who are generous in spirit are more likely to be true friends, rather than colleagues or casual business acquaintances. If you lack such supporters, you will have to take the risk of introducing yourself at events, and making cold calls.

Being prepared for rejection is advisable, until the atmosphere in your new domain warms up a bit. Any fresh marketing campaign or embarkation into forming partnerships requires managers to cultivate hyper-professional standards. Start fanning the warm glow of acceptance by learning about the business concerned. To achieve results, make an

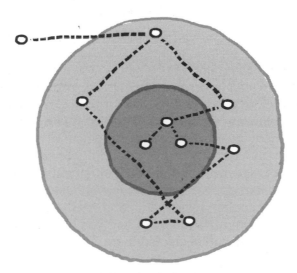

Figure 5.2 Moving out fo the comfort zone.

enthusiastic approach. This creates a good first impression, showing you to be well informed.

Observing the connections

As you move into unfamiliar surroundings it is likely that you will notice interesting facts about people. It may be that they studied at certain schools or colleges, worked for particular firms or are members of private clubs. I recall once seeing an image in glamour magazine *Vogue*. It was a diagram showing how everyone who had achieved notoriety or success in the fashion world connected. It was interesting to see how many had either studied at the top art schools at the same time, had worked with one another or were related to famous fashion designers. The further one travels in life, the more one understands that strategies for success can begin very early in life.

The question that requires asking is: 'If you don't have obvious factors in common with potential contacts, how you can become established within specific networks?' Without a recommendation, or achieving fame through accomplishment, it is difficult. Become as useful as possible to prospective contacts, without overly compromising your own interests, and develop a pretty determined outlook.

How to network

If you want to win friends, make it a point to remember them. The name sets the individual apart. The information we are imparting takes on a special importance when we approach the situation with the name of the individual.

Dale Carnegie, public speaking guru and author, 1888–1955

First, find out about networking events, and in the early years of business attend regularly. As your enterprise grows it is important to continue developing contacts, and not just at a senior level. I recall a very skilled commercial artist who was virtually bankrupt in his late 50s after running a small firm for many years. The reason he gave for the sorry state of affairs, after much thought about his situation, was that as he became older all his contacts slowly drifted off into retirement or had sadly died. What he wished he had done through his working life was form relationships with younger people, junior stylists and assistant art buyers. These people were his future commissioners – there had been plenty of chances to befriend them, and he had neglected them.

Second, be prepared to waste a few evenings or afternoons in fruitless quests. Even if you are sure specific people will be there, it can be the case that for some reason they fail to turn up. Even if you miss them, through absence or simply through lack of opportunity, you can still use this as a reason to make contact, beginning e-mails or phone calls with the phrase, 'I was hoping to get the chance to meet you last night', for example. The fact that you made the effort to go and get in touch will genuinely impress people. It demonstrates true initiative.

Third, during introductions, do remember people's names and positions. Forgetting simple details such as this can give the appearance of being incompetent and untrustworthy. Would you wish to work with people who could not retain the simplest facts in their minds?

To increase the prospect of others committing your name to memory, say it confidently as you make eye contact with them, smile and shake their hand. Every time a new person comes along, introduce yourself again, wear a name badge, and give them a business card before leaving, to emphasize the message! When trying to recollect other people's names there are several methods that can help:

- Say the person's name twice in your head, and every time you look at their face, say it again.
- Draw their name with a giant imaginary marker pen above their head.
- Make associations with their name, 'George' is wearing a 'green tie', 'Liz' is the same name as my 'best friend'; for 'Dawn Flowers' envisage a 'sunrise' and 'bouquet'.
- When listening to a large number of speakers at a conference, draw a small doodle about each of them in turn, possibly an impression of their hairstyle, shape of glasses, jewellery, colour of clothing or key comments made, and add their name. This makes it easy to identify them later, and impress them by being able to recall what they have said.
- If people offer a business card, make a quick note in a similar vein on it immediately afterwards. This will help you recall them even many years later.

The rules

Execute the appropriate follow-up. Often a seemingly successful trip will lead to nothing without adequate follow-up. Use meetings, trips, reports, and further communications to your best advantage.

William Julian King, professor of engineering and author, 1902–1983

The trick that one must learn with any type of networking, whether through business trips or the internet, is to keep contacts 'warm'. If many weeks or months have passed after making initial contact, it is possible people may not recall who you are and their interest in the proposal will have faded. So make sure after the first meeting that time is found to follow up on new leads, by phone and e-mail. Ask them, for instance, if they would like to receive newsletters, product offers or marketing materials, and invite them to interesting events.

Keeping in touch

If you are haunted by memories about distant broken promises 'to follow up', then it may not be too late. Think how to re-engage contacts after such a long period. Sending a personal note or card, even telephoning to say hello with the desire to 'catch up', can work wonders. Many small firms use long-arm tactics such as sending seasonal cards at Christmas time or in the New Year. Try not to be lazy by e-mailing 'virtual' cards with the justification of saving trees. Everyone knows there are plenty of printers who can offer cards made from recycled fibre.

Over the years, I have received cards electronically from companies that actually have just scanned a picture from the front of a card bought from a high street store. Digitally transmitting images without permission of the copyright owners, with no illustrator credit, can contravene copyright law. When I receive an e-mail with an embedded image such as this, it just conveys to me the sender either is naive about the law or lacks ethics. I'm not entirely sure which is worse.

Hosting parties for associates and clients at Christmas or celebrating business anniversaries is another worthwhile initiative. Including people, perhaps giving away useful or extravagant gifts, shows you not only remember but also value them. So what happens when you receive an invitation to a business event such as this? What are the rules of networking?

Face to face

I've got to go out and be social,
I've got to be bright and extremely polite,
And refrain from being too loose or too tight,
And mustn't impose conversational blight.

Noel Coward, entertainer and playwright, 1899–1973

When preparing to attend such an occasion, check the dress code. Bring professionally designed and printed business cards. Do not be amateurish and make your own. They are frontline marketing materials; cheap cards will not make the best impact. Invest in a smart compact box in which to store them. Tugging dog-eared cards from wallets hints at disorganization. As we will discuss in Chapter 10, 'How to present yourself', first impressions are fundamental.

As you arrive, the hosts usually stand at the door greeting guests, handing out name badges and a list of delegates. Make their acquaintance and thank them for organizing the event. If you are with a friend, it can make approaching people easier. If you are alone, it can be a bit nerve-racking. However, being unaccompanied allows you to be spontaneous and to engage as you wish. If there are no familiar faces, examine the guest list to see if there is anyone you could approach.

Alternatively go and stand in open spaces and smile. Don't cling to the nearest wall or hide behind a pillar. Hopefully, other lone visitors will come over to say hello. Always stretch out a hand and shake theirs – in most western countries this is an accepted custom. If a winning smile does not draw the crowds, go and stand near a cluster of people, and listen to the conversations. Make sure you are spotted hovering, and find a moment to interject with a positive comment, such as 'Yes, I agree with that'. Shortly afterwards, they will welcome you into the group.

When engagement commences, do try and listen to what people have to say. Ask them interested questions about what they do. After being asked about your own business or role, don't waffle on endlessly. Be clear and concise about what is special about your products and services.

Networking is predominantly not about making friends. It is more about the chance of creating alliances (Hill 2007). Some of the people you meet will indeed become friends. You should bear in mind this is not the reason why you are there. Yes, it is important to socialize and be cordial, but that is not the main objective. Sometimes encountering people like yourself is so absorbing that 30 minutes can easily pass by, with the consequence of failing to converse with any of the other 100 representatives. One must keep an eye on the clock.

A few cautionary words

The people you converse with could be future competitors. So think carefully before answering probing questions, especially about market research, industry know-how and specialist suppliers. I have observed many occasions when commercially sensitive information has been given away to the underhand opportunist.

Exiting gracefully

One way of moving on is to form a mini-partnership with someone you have struck up a rapport with and explore the event together. Another approach is to wait until others come over to chat, and then smoothly depart, exchange business cards and offer to follow up, perhaps phoning or e-mailing a useful article or information about your services. An alternative method in parting company is to say that you need to talk to a colleague who has just dashed out of room. This always gives the option of returning to this person later. Another exit strategy is mentioning the need to leave early, adding that you have enjoyed getting to know them, but 'just have to catch a few people' before you go.

Always say good-bye to people that you have met when finally exiting. This is not simply a matter of good manners, but shows how much you valued making their acquaintance.

Closing thoughts

Alliances for business, professional and economic advancement, consisting of individuals who have a personal motive in connection with the object of alliance.

Napoleon Hill, author, 1883–1970

Success in business is achieved by forming alliances or by simply making friends in the industry. The chances of getting a 'break' or gaining worthwhile opportunities will be greatly improved if you gain assistance from the right people.

Key points

- Identify key figures in your sector that you would like to meet.
- Start to research into successful people and businesses in your industry.
- Decide what you would like to achieve from talking to them.
- Find out about networking events, talks or conferences that will be useful to attend.

- Practise introducing yourself, summing up your business in 30 seconds.
- Think about how you can be helpful to new contacts and interesting ways to conduct a follow-up.

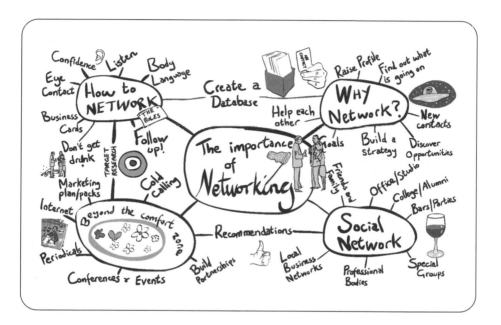

Enterprise skills booster

- If you are starting up a business, create a mind map® of all the people you currently know.
- Divide them into segments: social, work, college, customers, suppliers, etc.
- If you are a larger firm, make headed sections in your database and add the details of all current contacts.
- On a fresh piece of paper, write down the names of three people you would like to meet and why.
- Do you know anyone who may know these people? If not, what will be your next step?

- Is there a magazine that may be interested in publishing an interview with an entrepreneur? Could you be an impromptu Michael Parkinson or Oprah Winfrey? Contact your favourite periodical and put in a proposal to the editor. If they agree, this may be a chance to get to meet one of your three key people.
- Think of 10 questions you would like to know the answer to.
- Use the internet to find similar businesses to your own in different countries.
- E-mail them and ask them if they would be willing to have a chat with you about how they have cultivated clients and databases.
- Compare and contrast their experiences with your own.

6

Knowing your customer

If there were dreams to sell
What would you buy?

Thomas Lovell Beddoes, poet and playwright, 1803–1849

Discovering what the customer desires is the first step in the sales process. It is important to identify the best approach to selling by familiarizing yourself with the customer's mindset. This can be achieved by finding out as much as possible about them, including their dreams in the form of aspiration: what they want and why.

Before making any presentations or marketing plans you need to understand the reasons why people make the choices they do. Prosperous businesses spend an enormous amount of time, not just satisfying clients, but cultivating interest and demand. They are able to build market share as they appreciate what their customers value.

In this chapter we will focus upon methods, strategies and skills that any entrepreneur or salesperson would find useful to improve their ability to sell. We start by learning more about our current and future customers.

The uncurious entrepreneur

An entrepreneur began an outsized women's lingerie business, selling underwear from a website. The business was losing vast sums of money so the entrepreneur sought advice. The adviser was mystified about what was going wrong with the business. Customers had purchased items from the website and no garments had been returned, nor complaints made, yet there was rarely a repeat order.

When the adviser saw the garment packaging that was being sent to the customer by post, she realized where the entrepreneur had gone wrong. It was gaudy, with 'size 18–28' blazoned in a luminous colour across the front. Customers were being put off from re-ordering due to sheer embarrassment.

The entrepreneur had failed to undertake elementary research and interview potential customers before spending large sums of money on unsuitable branding. By overlooking the sensitivities of the customers, the company paid a heavy price.

Who is your customer?

To satisfy the customer is the mission and purpose of every business.

Peter Drucker, business guru and author, 1909–2005

The four questions you should ask before undertaking any business venture are:

- Who will your customers be?
- Why will they wish to buy?
- Where are they?
- What are they willing to pay?

Find out the answers before investing substantial amounts of time and money, a great deal of which can be wasted in product development and promotion when elementary research is not undertaken. A common mistake, especially in artistic and innovative initiatives, is developing a product before thoroughly investigating the marketplace.

Understanding consumers

Large popular design firms such as IKEA® think about the manufacturing process in reverse. If a popular price range for a lamp is £7.99 for instance, their designers will have to produce a lamp that will retail at this price. Most students going through art and design colleges are sheltered from the realities of how to make money from their creative products. They do not understand the fact that to make a profit they have to cost the entire process and not just slap a price tag on at the end. They harbour a misplaced hope that customers will magically appear and be willing to pay the prices asked.

There are many overly idealistic entrepreneurs, not just artists, who sleep-walk into this kind of disaster. Lacking rational thought, they embark on an enthusiastic mission to make an idea happen without thinking through market demand and financial viability.

Is there sufficient demand?

If you desire to make money from business, then you have to be confident about market demand. If there isn't a ready market, be pretty sure you can cultivate one. Then be prepared to initiate a high-risk, high-cost entrepreneurial venture. It is important to realize that this type of approach to launching products and services is usually only attempted with a great deal of financial backing and expertise. Take the example of budget airlines, which nowadays we all take for granted. There was nothing like them in the airline industry before Freddie Laker pioneered the concept in the 1970s with his 'Air Bus'. More recently in the UK, no one was initially interested in 3G mobile phones when they first came out. Then Vodafone launched the phones with the assistance of David Beckham. This was an expensive high-cost advertising campaign that did pay off by stimulating demand.

Develop an inquiring mind

The object of a salesman is not to make sales, but to make customers.

Mary Kay Ash, founder of Mary Kay Cosmetics, 1918–2001

It is extremely important to understand who your customers are, and where they are located. How can you begin to negotiate a business deal or plan a marketing campaign if you don't know at whom or where to aim it?

There are many general ways of gathering information about possible customers or clients, such as paying for marketing advice from consult-ants, market research reports, mailing lists, industry directories or gaining quantitative free information on statistics and detailed demographic infor-mation from reputable websites. More qualitative methods are conduct-ing surveys or talking to focus groups. **The most important element in finding out more about your target market is to ask potential customers the right questions**. You have to understand their needs and expectations as well as gather basic information. If for example you are selling products or services from a website, how will potential customers find you? Will they keyword search using a search engine, use an online directory or look through *Yellow Pages*?

Collecting customer details is important if you never meet them face to face, especially when selling through catalogues or via the internet. When trading from a distance, it is vital to persuade purchasers to provide as much information about themselves as possible within reason. This will help to improve marketing techniques and encourage repeat orders.

Introductory steps in face-to-face selling

If you have the luxury of meeting potential customers face to face in your shop or at a fair, how do you find out more about them? The first thing to do when noticing a visitor is to let them browse for a short time before making an approach. Then, armed with a smile, greet them with a 'Hello'. Consider different types of opening questions to gather useful information about them.

Is it this first time you have visited this fair?

This type of question is invaluable. If they answer 'no', then ask them how they found out about the event and why they have come. If they answer 'yes', and you keep quiet and listen then perhaps they will reveal who they are. If useful information is not forthcoming, then follow through, with further questions, such as:

- What are you interested in buying?
- Is this the first time you have bought this product?
- Is it for yourself or are you shopping for a friend?
- Would you like to see our new product range?
- Do your own a store?
- Are you a buyer?
- Oh, you are from the 'X periodical/media'; would you like a press pack?
- Would you like to place an order today?
- Is this within your budget?
- How did you find out about us?
- Who recommended us to you?
- As a buyer for this particular store, what sort of quantities would interest you?

- So you are a *runner* for a *buyer;* would they like a brochure and a free sample?
- You may be interested in these other product lines?
- Would you like a brochure, or perhaps come to our next product launch?
- I'll just make a note of your address and contact details?

Find out more

You need to establish who your customer is through friendly discussion and subtle fact-finding. This will help prepare your sales pitch. Consider:

- In business there may be several types of customers.
- It could be that you trade with other businesses and corporate firms.
- You may sell goods to individual consumers or direct to store owners as well as taking orders from professional buyers.
- Businesses often act as suppliers to public sector bodies such as schools, colleges, sports centres, hospitals, prisons and local authorities.
- Some entrepreneurs and small businesses may employ agents or other intermediaries such as freelance salespeople.
- Others may rely on sponsorship for particular ventures.

It may be the case that your marketing campaign has to target one customer who is the beneficiary, and appeal to another who pays. In promoting a business one has to bear in mind there could be several types of customers and beneficiaries. Figure 6.1 depicts a business that sells children's toys. This is a good example of complex marketing issues, showing how two customers need pleasing, though only one pays.

Is your customer who you think they are?

When venturing into business for the first time it can be easy to misunderstand who the customer is and target the wrong sector completely. Other errors include misrepresenting the product or service, and mismatching methods of communication with the target audience.

A good example of a mismatch is a man I met who set up a service to ensure speedy delivery of lost front door keys to those locked out of their homes. His plan was to make a short sales pitch to guests at business

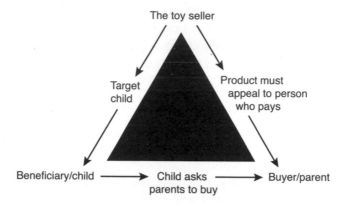

The toy seller

Target child

Product must appeal to person who pays

Beneficiary/child ——————▶ Child asks ——————▶ Buyer/parent
parents to buy

Figure 6.1 Targeting more than one market

networking events. It was obvious he had started his business without conducting basic research into his target market. His customers would not be there, among the well organized and focused. All he was achieving in this direct approach was to irritate people.

The type of customer he needed to reach was the absentminded commuter, shopper or clubber. A good way to communicate with the forgetful and disorganized would be through placing posters in window spaces near key-cutters, railway stations and lost property offices, or advertising spaces in minicabs or on the back of toilet doors in bars. Other ideas could be creating promotional merchandise in the form of key fobs, to give away to likely punters outside clubs and from high street key-cutters.

Understanding the mind of customers

Find out what the client's real objective is.

Paul Arden, art director and author, 1940–2008

Once you have established who and where the clients or customers are, you can explore further what their desires are. A good starting point is to ask them why they have chosen you or this particular product. This can also help in confirming the effectiveness of current marketing strategies. Is it because your business was recommended by another? Had the client spotted an advert in the local paper or feature in a magazine?

Next, assess if the client or customer is pressurized due to time constraints. The strain and pace of their voice usually gives this away. As mentioned in Chapter 11, 'Negotiating a better deal', this could affect your bargaining position regarding price. The client may be willing to pay more for a quick service or immediate delivery. When dealing with clients, especially new ones, there can be an element of risk. You may not trust them to pay. To minimize this possibility, you could request to credit check them, or agree payment up front.

Use questions to guide your own mindset about the customer's objectives:

● Would they like tips or advice about the products or service?
● Are they open to ideas about what the service should include or how they would like to purchase your goods?
● Have you discovered what their desire is?
● How much do they have to spend?
● Most importantly, what don't they want?

This last point is particularly interesting. You might be able to persuade customers to choose you over competitors. This is why it is worth investing time to fully understand the marketplace. Do this by comparing your prices and quality of products or services to that of other suppliers. You will be able to argue a case. If the customer has a tight budget, for instance, you can demonstrate what good value your offer is in contrast to those of other more expensive and perhaps less suitable suppliers.
Useful types of phrases to use when trying to persuade customers:

● This product was recently voted best buy of the month in *Get it* magazine.
● Our services were recently featured in *Top Recommended* periodical last month.
● Our stockists include Habitat, Harvey Nichols and Peter Jones.
● We provide consultancy to Ideo, Virgin, Coca-Cola® and others.
● Oh yes, you may have seen (mention celebrity's name) brought one from us yesterday…
● Yes, you could try visiting 'Y' but you may find they are more expensive.
● Yes, you could try contacting 'Z', though we can guarantee delivery today.
● No problem, we can do it now.
● If you buy today, we can offer you a special discount.

- Here, have a free sample/we can offer you a free 15-minute consultancy.
- We are the first to get these products in the country.
- This line of products is only available from us.
- All our products are ethically sourced/fair-trade/made from recycled materials.

Value to the customer

In my factory we make cosmetics, but in my stores we sell hope.

Charles Revson, founder of Revlon®, 1906–1975

Before we move on to learning how to sell, it is vital we understand what is of value to the customer. There are thousands of reasons why people and businesses decide to purchase products and services from shops or suppliers. We will start by analysing six key themes. For ease of explanation, I will refer to all services or goods for sale as 'the product'.

1. Purpose and use

Does the customer really want to buy?

Could it be they would simply like to hire, lease or license the product? With expensive machines for example, a business or an individual may only need to use them occasionally, and may prefer to hire them at particular times of the year. A company may want to use photographs or artwork for marketing purposes or to hang on the walls in their premises. However, they don't want to pay huge fees. The creative professional could loan artworks to them, or offer a licence, so that the business can reproduce images for short periods of time.

Buy land, they're not making it anymore.

Mark Twain, humorist and writer, 1835–1910

2. Availability versus exclusivity

What will encourage customers to buy?

Is 'exclusivity' really about understanding customers' aspirations? That the product is viewed as specialized or luxurious, reflective of economic prosperity or simply glamorous? Thus, are they willing to pay more for privileged access or a limited edition?

Equally, availability may be important to consumers so they have time to take advantage of the offer, collect products, make repeat orders or save up to make a purchase. It is worth thinking about whether your sales will be aimed at a rich minority (high priced/exclusive) or the vast majority of the population who take home average incomes (good value/availability).

3. Spending and return

What does the customer gain in return?

People always like bargains, free offers, trial prices, introductory or two-for-one offers, and buying goods in sales. When they decide to spend, what are they getting in return? Will they be saving money on items or making an extra purchase? During recessions or 'credit crunches', consumers may make more economical decisions, either making special purchases or more rational ones. For example, a 'special' purchase may be a treat or a present for a loved one; this may make buyers feel 'happy' as they spend. A rational transaction would be making a multifunctional purchase, such as buying a bag that will match several outfits. This type of purchase gives the customer a sense of 'achievement', through solving a problem by making an astute purchase.

4. Specialist knowledge and connection

Would it help customers if they had extra information?

Some customers would value the chance to ask questions about the product when making a purchase. If you are not able to help your customers, they will become frustrated and decide not to buy. You should be able to respond either as the 'voice of the expert', or perhaps in a more personal way by referring to your own experience, or feedback from other customers. To make a 'connection' and build rapport with a customer requires skilled judgement.

5. Worth and importance

What is of value to the customer?

- Is the customer buying this product to improve profit margins, by investing in equipment or services that will save them time and money, or improve productivity?

- Could it be that the product is improving the quality of life of the suppliers through fair-trade initiatives? Will it reduce customers' carbon footprint? This could fit with their ethical beliefs, or prompt a purchase made simply to comply with regulations.
- Are they buying the product to improve their education or skills, enhance their life or environment?
- Is it to make them feel happy or solve a problem?
- Is it because customers desire to own a product that others don't have, or alternatively are they relieved that the product is always on sale?
- Are they looking to save money, through negotiation, or simply hunting for a bargain?

6. Trust and reputation

Is the customer risk averse?

Building trust and offering a product repeatedly to a consistent standard is usually an important factor in the customer's mind. If potential customers hear from others that the quality of your product varies or is substandard, this will put them off. Getting good press and dealing quickly with unsatisfied customers can stop the spread of rumours. The critical will only be able to gossip about how well your business sorted out a problem. Building a reputation can take time. It will reduce customer uncertainty and build immediate trust if you gain product endorsements from other reputable firms or high-profile customers.

Closing thoughts

The hardest thing to do is see what is right in front of your eyes.

Johann Wolfgang von Goethe, poet and novelist, 1749–1832

Try not to rush or skip this analysis of your customers. Research can throw up simple solutions such as offering services at slightly different times or products in other colours and sizes. If you are an idealist you may discover there is a mismatch between what you wish to offer and what customers are willing to buy. Be prepared to modify what you intend to sell or even change the idea completely to fit the demand.

Key points

- Question as many people and business owners as possible to assess market demand, before embarking on selling products or services.

- If you are already in business and experiencing problems, why not invest in gaining the opinion of a professional business adviser or marketer?

- Why not hold a feedback meeting with your sales force, and speak with customers directly to see how you can gain a better understanding of the situation? Find out what works and what doesn't.

- You might have to adopt different approaches to customers, especially if seeking to satisfy more than one market.

- Start to develop a number of useful opening questions for developing a sales pitch.

- Through research, find out what is of value to the customer. How will this information be used to improve marketing materials, presentation, packaging and your sales pitch?

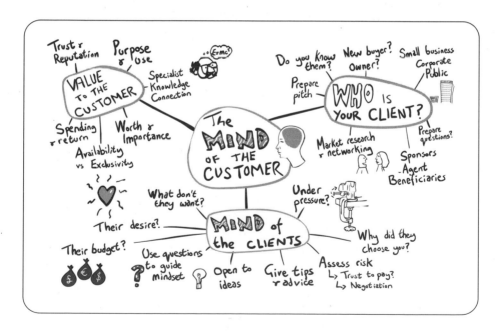

Enterprise skills booster

- Go out and find out what products or services there is a demand for today.
- Consider your own actions as a customer; what are your reasons for buying products or services?
- What do you think people would like to buy in two years' time? Four years? Six years? Jot down some ideas, and do some more research to test their feasibility.
- If starting up or currently in business, draft out a mind map® and write down facts and thoughts about your future or current customers. Then consider how you would find out whether your assumptions are valid.
- While you are gaining feedback, make additional enquiries:
  - Why do customers choose to buy from you?
  - Is there anything wrong with the product or service?
  - How would they like products or services to be improved?
  - Do you think your customers may be interested in other products or services you could offer?
  - What would encourage them to place further or bigger orders?

7

How to sell

Good salesmen, like good cooks, create an appetite when the buyer doesn't seem to be hungry.

George Horace Lorimer, editor and novelist, 1868–1937

Preparing a sales pitch is like finding ingredients to make a tasty cake. Getting the sales process right takes a great deal of skill and preparation. Trust with the customer is created through having an assortment of components in place. Only then will it result in customers happily hiring or buying. As we will discuss in Chapter 10, 'How to present yourself', there are a range of different selling contexts: presenting, pitching and networking. Having a poorly thought-through sales process is like failing to observe the rudiments of baking. If a cake has no visual or aromatic appeal, quite simply the customer won't want it.

As in the previous chapter, for ease of explanation, I will refer to services or goods for sale as the 'product'.

The sales process

Successful salesmanship is 10 per cent preparation and 90 per cent presentation.

Bertrand R Canfield, author and lecturer, 1898–1969

Positive thinking, personal presentation and the quality of your voice are the first elements to consider. If you are feeling frustrated or fragile, this will be noticed by others from your voice and facial expressions. Positive thinking can help, even in the most difficult of situations. However, if you are suffering a bad day, perhaps take a break, and return when the batteries are recharged.

Try to avoid speaking quickly when talking to customers. Rushing through content doesn't work in any situation. Avoid giving the impression you are reading from a script, and don't over-rehearse what you say. People are more comfortable with spontaneous interaction. The tone of your voice is so important to get right. Recently, when a salesman cold-called me to make a sales pitch, his voice was so flat and even in tone, that I felt I was talking to a robot. He exuded no personal warmth or charm, essential qualities for selling.

Be engaging and friendly when approaching customers. When you are on a stand at a trade fair, don't just sit there watching people wander past. You need to be on your feet. Invest in a high stool, so when you wish to rest for a few minutes, at least you can maintain a good height level to make eye contact. Smile at people, say hello, and ask them opening questions. Don't make judgements about the way customers dress. Many wealthy people dress down when embarking on buying sprees. Being festooned in high-class tailoring or ostentatious 'bling' may not be helpful to a negotiation process.

Distance selling

If you are planning to sell goods and services via a website, it is worth exploring the technicalities of search engine optimization. One of the essential tasks to get right is selecting appropriate words for the 'Meta Tag' (25 words that describe your business activities) that you have to register with search engines. A customer who searches using a search engine will type in words, and the search facility will show up your website somewhere – it may be on page 1 or 1,000. What you need to achieve is getting your website to come up in the first page or two of search results. There are countless methods of optimizing your website presence and attracting customers to your site. It is worth hiring experienced web designers or e-commerce consultants who have specialized knowledge, rather than attempting to do it all yourself.

Constructing a USP

Each advertisement must say to each reader:
'Buy this product, and you will get this specific benefit'.
The proposition must be so strong it can move the mass millions...
These three points are summed up in the phrase: UNIQUE SELLING PROPOSITION.
This is a USP.

Rosser Reeves, advertising agent, 1910–1984

The unique selling point (USP) is a vital part of selling a product. Why should customers choose you and not your competitors? There is an old saying: 'In a field of grass you will never find two blades the same.' You really have to figure out what makes your product the best or unique in the marketplace. Usually, businesses will put their USP or slogan on marketing materials. This is useful, but in selling you need to verbalize it naturally in conversation. (For assistance with constructing a USP, see the exercises in the 'Enterprise skills booster' section, at the end of this chapter.)

The importance of branding

Branding is ownership of part of the mind. If you are a business, you need to be in the minds of people you do business with.

Roddy Mullin, marketing consultant and author, 1945–

Branding and design are important ingredients in the sales recipe. As mentioned in Chapter 5, 'The importance of networking', good-quality well-designed promotional materials are essential. A memorable brand name and identity will have a strong impact on consumers. Don't try to be your own designer, unless you are qualified in the subject. Employ the services of a professional designer or commercial artist, especially one who has experience in your industry sector. Look for designers who have good client lists and a track record of creating brands.

Large firms or team-enterprises will be able to afford the services of more established art or design agencies. Agencies will not only develop your brand, but can create media advertising campaigns. Remember when developing any brand to make sure you inform the designer that you wish to trademark the business or product name and logo. Don't waste your time with designers who don't understand about brand development. Their competence is displayed in their portfolio, showcasing previous creative ideas that have acquired trademark status.

How to structure a sales pitch

Marketing is figuring out who your customers and prospects are and how to get their business.
Selling is what you do once you've established contact with customers or prospects.

Jay Goltz, CEO Glotz group and author, 1956–

Once the mindset of your customer has been established, the basic sales process is made up of four elements.

1. Raise interest or excitement

Researching the minds of your customers will arm you with clues about their aspirations and desires. Cultivating useful phrases you can sprinkle into conversation will be invaluable. Include words such as 'new', 'latest model', 'award-winning', 'feedback from customers suggests', 'specialist', 'expert', 'limited' 'offer' and 'free'. The product may help customers to solve a problem, save time, effort or money, enhance business performance, or improve the quality of their life in some way.

2. Address any doubts or concerns (reduce risk)

This is when you can mention your company's 'returns policy' or 'guarantee'. Other useful phrases are 'trial periods', 'free samples', 'full refund', 'replacement within 24 hours', 'thoroughly tested', 'help line', 'no problem' and 'get back to me any time'. Perhaps mention, if true, that there have been no returns or complaints so far.

3. Confirm how desires or expectations will be fulfilled

You must be honest and believe in your product. Be truthful to customers, don't make disingenuous claims; they are not idiots. If step two of the sales process is working, and any fears are allayed, you can then illuminate the way the product will fulfil their expectations. It is best to have your own thoughts, but consider phrases similar to, 'independent research suggests', 'I think it will work', 'it should last at least 10 years', 'you will notice an improvement', 'yes I agree it suits you', 'other clients or customers have found', 'this has been popular', 'it's a wise move' or 'it's a good choice for you'.

4. Where and how to buy – available now, from stockists, or a website

Hopefully by now the customer is warmed up. It is likely they would like to buy. Other incentives to offer up front or bring into play later include, 'limited offers', 'discount', 'vouchers', 'free delivery', 'no extra costs' and 'three for two'.

To encourage further spending, you could incentivize customers by having an introductory offer of 'extra products' or a 'free gift' if they spend over a certain amount. Alternatively, if indirectly selling via the media, you can direct potential customers to local stockists or purchase via a website.

Until trust in the product has been established, there won't be any repeat orders. Therefore, it is important to check, if possible, why customers don't make further orders in the future.

One last thought about closing a sale is to avoid discounting if you can. (Sometimes this is unavoidable.) **It may make more economic sense to offer more products or an additional service then reduce prices.** For example, if a retailer requests a 15 per cent discount then in real terms this is a substantial cut in your profit margin. Remember retailers will mark up products anywhere from 100 to 400 per cent. If you offered them 5 per cent more product instead of discounting, then they would easily make some extra profit (for more about this topic see the penultimate point in the 'Customer not happy?' section further on in this chapter).

Practical things to think about

> I could go out and sell £10 notes for £9 each all day long with no problem I can tell you! But even I wouldn't make a profit.
>
> Sir Alan Sugar, businessman, 1947–

Underpinning the topics outlined so far are other issues that need to be firmly in place to achieve excellence in completing a sale.

Ethical considerations

Whether conscientiously, as a selling point or in the light of regulatory requirements, a number of ethical matters have to be taken into account. Such issues range from environmental concerns to social responsibility. Make sure that ethical concerns feature in your pitch, labelling and other marketing materials.

Complying with the law

Trading standards, consumer rights, advertising standards authority, health and safety, environmental regulations, distance selling regulations, terms and conditions, contracts...

Understand what your obligations are within the laws that apply to these areas, especially if selling at distance by mail order or the internet. As every year goes by, businesses are required to be more careful about how they describe their products, any claims they make and the way they are advertised.

Your products may have to be subjected to testing and approval by environmental and safety bodies before they can be legally sold. Merchandise may require clear labelling such as the 'price', 'includes/excludes VAT', 'ingredients', 'fibre' or 'material content', 'instructions for use', and 'safety' or 'hazard warnings'. When selling, make sure you have terms and conditions, explaining your liabilities and the rights of the customer. Having your own professional documents such as order forms, invoice systems and methods of issuing receipts is crucial. All these matters should be understood and in place at the start of trading.

Pricing and presentation

You can't have a quality product for sale at a low price. You may be able to offer good value at a low price, but not a specialist or premium product.

Pricing is very important to the perception of value by the consumer. Getting it right is vital. I have met many people in business who don't charge enough for their products or services. This is either though a lack of confidence to charge the market rate, or through failure to take into account all the expenses incurred in making the product or delivering the service.

Avoid undercutting

Sometimes being 'cheap' will not make you money in the end. I recall a friend musing about the sale of his car. He wanted to get rid of it quickly so he advertised it for a few hundred pounds. It didn't sell. So he re-advertised it with an extra zero on the end of the original price. It sold straight away. The first price was simply too inexpensive, and people must have thought there was something wrong with the car. In business, there will always be less costly products in the marketplace, but it is unlikely they can offer any real quality or consistency.

Market demand

Market demand is important; if there isn't any, can you afford to spend time and effort cultivating it? **Most successful business people find out through research what people want, and then sell it to them!** Being prepared to negotiate prices up rather than down is another element to thinking through the whole process. Try not to view securing cut-price volume sales as a success. All that is achieved is undermining market value, and forcing you and your business colleagues to work harder to produce more products for smaller profit margins. If suppliers' prices, transport or other cost should go up, then a loss may well be incurred. Focus on profit not the volume.

However, in particular sales contexts such as downloading virtual products from the internet – current examples include music or purchasing licences to reproduce images (i-stock) – the 'pile 'em high and sell 'em cheap' approach can work well, as there are few costs in terms of labour and overheads.

Availability

Presentation in relation to availability is crucial. If you are trying to make money through offering 'exclusivity' such as limited or special editions, then your presentation should reflect this. I recall a market trader who was selling imported hand-decorated ceramic tableware on a small market stall. He had followed my advice by displaying the china in small groups, placed on silk, to convey a sense of quality. Then he wrecked it by clumsily stacking hundreds of cups and tableware in piles at the back of the stall, all in full view of customers. His ill-thought-through storage methods sent a powerful message out to customers: here is a 'job lot' of crockery of little worth and value.

Customer not happy?

Don't stand for shoddy service. If you're not being served, walk out.

Mary Portas, author and retail consultant, 1962–

Try not to lose a sale by ignoring customers or not having enough staff to attend to them. The quote by Mary Portas above refers to retail situations, but the same principle applies to selling by phone, internet or direct mail. To build a client base or market share you need to be able to cope with enquiries or demand.

The customer is always right.

Shop slogan of Harry Gordon, owner of Selfridges, 1858–1947

It is essential to realize the customer may not always be right. However, solutions still have to found to placate the discontented. You don't want to unnecessarily annoy people, especially in the present day with mass communication open to all. It is easy for ex-customers to express disgruntlement on a global scale via e-mail, in chat rooms or notice boards, and via online social networking.

So here is a step-by-step plan to deal with unhappy customers:

1. Be prepared for objections, and build in systems to deal with complaints.
2. When a customer complains, find out what is wrong and listen without interrupting them, unless it is to clarify understanding.
3. Try to sound sympathetic and show you understand the problem.
4. Don't come back at the customer with comments like, 'no one else has complained' or 'you are the only one to complain'. It will not resolve the situation, and may cause the customer to become even more annoyed.
5. Consider carefully before making an apology. If it is a simple problem, for instance if the customer has been sent the 'wrong product', or 'it doesn't work', it's the 'wrong size or colour', 'product not arrived', then issuing an apology is something you should do straight away. If a genuine mistake has been made, apologize and then follow the complaints system, for example replacing the item or resending the product.
6. However, if the problem is serious, for instance if the product has caused a serious 'loss of custom or money', or the product was found to be a 'fake' or a 'copy', or more importantly it has caused an injury or death, **then do not issue any apology**. Don't say or do anything, before seeking the advice of a solicitor or lawyer. If you apologize it can be viewed, should the matter go to court, as admitting liability, which could have all kinds of consequences for your business.
7. Dealing with difficult but not serious complaints, you should always inform the customer how long it will take to resolve: a few minutes or days. Always make sure you send customers a letter acknowledging their complaint and later expressing the hope that the resolution has been satisfactory.
8. A letter may not be necessary if the complaint is not serious and can be solved quickly.
9. If, after listening, you are certain their objections have no foundation you may wish to reason with the customer. Try to get them to value what they have, point out how your product compares with others available in the marketplace. Demonstrating that what they have is a good deal may sway them a little, and encourage them to withdraw the complaint.

10. Another issue is making refunds. (Laws concerning the rights of customers vary around the world, so please check the regulations about the time periods within which traders are under a legal obligation to issue a refund if the customer demands it. Equally, it is worth checking at what point the right of customers to demand any refund or replacement expires.)

Avoid making cash refunds to dissatisfied customers if you can, as it may be a less expensive option to replace or remake the product. For instance, I recall a company that sold rugs. The company imported the rugs from abroad at a unit price of £50 each and retailed them for £300. The problem was that occasionally a small number of the rugs were substandard and this wasn't obvious until they had been walked on for a few hours. When dissatisfied customers brought their slightly threadbare rugs back, the directors immediately refunded them the money, without considering any alternative forms of compensation.

I suggested that it would be better to offer them a replacement rug, or even two for the drivers of a hard bargain. Instead of losing a gross profit of £250 by refunding the money, they would only lose a further £50–£100 in the form of replacement rugs. The customer could view the offer of an extra rug as a bonus and might prefer this to a complete refund. This is a good example of keeping your customers happy.

Closing thoughts

Any fool can paint a picture, but it takes a wise man to be able to sell it.

Samuel Butler, novelist, 1835–1902

As will be explained in the next chapter, sales can take time to complete. An important aspect of selling is to focus on profit rather than pursuing a policy of volume sales, discounting or doing extra work outside an agreed contract. It is wise to remember the power of dissatisfied customers, and it is worth being proactive in finding a speedy resolution and not to simply ignore complaints.

Key points

● Think through your entire presentation of your product and sales process. Get help to devise a USP, both a written and verbal version.
● Make sure you get the pricing of your product right.

- Develop systems for dealing with complaints that are written down so new employees can understand and refer to them. Founding members of businesses amass a great deal of knowledge over time. New staff can't easily access what is stored in your memory. They will need all the procedures about your methods of selling and dealing with complaints presented to them in a simple and accessible way.

- Invest in brand development in the form of design and trademark protection.

- Get the legal stuff right, whatever it is – try to avoid falling foul of regulations.

- Prepare yourself for objections and complaints, and options outside the standard refund for compensating the dissatisfied.

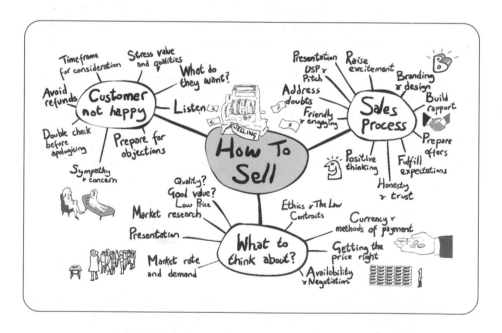

Enterprise skills booster

- Start to draft out a mind map® of your current or future sales process.
- This will need to be summoned up in the form of a step plan to enable you and others to learn how to pitch a sale.
- Have a go at selling some of your own possessions that you no longer need. Try selling them at local car boot sales or markets, or on eBay™. It may turn out to be a useful experience!
- To construct a USP think through all the key 'features' of your product or service. List two to three facts, if you wish, picked from Table 7.1.
- Now think about the 'benefits' to the customer. List two to three benefits, if you wish, picked from Table 7.2.
- Now have a go at writing a short sentence about your business, using one or two selected words from your 'features' and 'benefits' lists.
- Your brand embodies these values. Go and research more established businesses similar to your own. Find out if the logo or trademark they currently use is the same as when they first started. If it has changed, establish why they made the change.
- Start collecting examples of other businesses marketing materials and images of any business logos you find interesting. You should find these materials a useful resource when you start to brand or rebrand your business.

Table 7.1 Features

What are the key facts concerning your business, products or services?

Specialist	Expert	Professional	Bespoke	Handmade
New material	Exclusive	Ethically sourced	Fair trade	Ergonomic
Recycled	Organic	Award winning	Prize winning	Best voted
Low priced	Good value	Local	Efficient	Quality
Frequent	Innovative solution	Low cost	Made in Britain	First or new

Table 7.2 Benefits
Reasons customers should buy?

Save money	Save time	Save energy	Save space	Cut down bills
Reduce carbon footprint	Affordable	Bargain	Efficiency	Increase sales
Improve performance	Reliability	Reduce risks	Long lasting	Convenient
Feel fantastic	Look great	Help you relax	Make a unique gift	Complete a collection
Great entertainment	For all the community	Enhance your environment	Beautiful addition	Feel safe

8

Managing time wisely

A man who dares to waste one hour of time has not discovered the value of life.

Charles Darwin, author and theorist, 1809–1882

As people get older they begin to realize that time is more precious than money. It is usually possible to replace what we spend, but never to reinstate lost time. Try to avoid wasting time. It is a finite resource.

When hearing the phrase 'this is costing me time and money', you may not have given it a second thought. With some further pondering, you will realize that the phrase is encapsulating, quite literally, the point that time has a worth, in terms of monetary significance. When starting out in business, understanding how to 'cost' time is a basic financial planning exercise. Entrepreneurs must learn about the art of money management. However, we won't be covering the technicalities of basic financial planning in this book. We will approach the subject in a different way by exploring how we value and make use of time.

The dreamy freelancer

A firm offered a freelancer a year's contract. When the owner of the business asked her for her daily rate, she replied she would work two days a week for 40 per cent of £40,000 per annum.

The owner then proceeded to divide £40,000 by 365 days, making a daily rate of £109. The freelancer was a bit confused, as she expected the rate to be higher. She was naïve about pricing, so decided the calculation must be correct and accepted it.

Of course, what she should have done was calculate that she would work approximately 80 days over 48 weeks – 40 per cent of £40,000 is £16,000; then divide £16,000 by 80 days, which makes a daily rate of £200.

It was only after attending a business start-up course that she realized she had been duped. Understanding costing and pricing ratios are fundamental principles of money management, without which you will not make any profit from your venture.

Managing a year

I was born and then the next day I was 40.

Tallulah Bankhead, film actress, 1902–1968

Whether writing your first business plan or managing a number of employees, it is important to be realistic about what can be achieved in a day, week, month, season or year. To find out if a business venture is going to be profitable, you need to work out how long orders or schedules of work take to complete and what resources will be needed: people, materials, machines and so on. Accurate costing and pricing is not just considering a direct ratio between time and money, as there are many other elements to consider.

It can be very complicated to estimate the time needed to deliver a service or make a product. If a business owner or manager gets these calculations wrong, by overestimating the time and resources required, the completed work will come in under budget, resulting in a large profit. Equally, time and resources may have been underestimated, meaning the completed project is over budget. In this case, inaccurate costing will cause the business to make a loss.

Time is the scarcest resource and unless it is managed nothing else can be managed.

Peter Drucker, business guru and author, 1909–2005

The fundamental element is time. You need to make use of time as efficiently as possible, to maximize money-making potential. It can be useful, when planning, to draft a timeline on a long piece of paper. This can be a helpful tool for designing effective schedules; see Figure 8.1. Ask yourself what are the critical tasks in your project. If fundamental tasks are not completed within deadlines then everything else is knocked back. This can

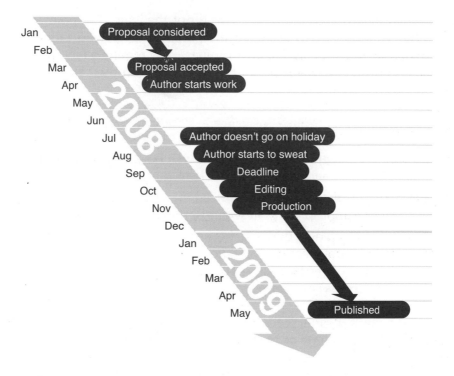

Figure 8.1 Timeline

cause a business extra expense or even a failure to accomplish its targets. It is important to define key points or stages in the project this will make it easier to measure progress. There will always be other minor tasks that can be completed late, without affecting the next stage in the process.

How time is used

Annual income twenty pounds, annual expenditure nineteen nineteen six, result happiness. Annual income twenty pounds, annual expenditure twenty pounds nought and six, result misery.

Mr Wilkins Micawber, a character in *David Copperfield*, by Charles Dickens, novelist, 1812–1870

The calculations in Figures 8.2 to 8.6 are an introduction to help you understand the ratio of business to leisure time, which is a key factor in improving money management skills. Arguably, you may work all hours of the day and night and never stop! Most entrepreneurs do work tirelessly in the first few years of setting up a business, and many managers work more than their contracted hours. This is not the issue. The point is how does the input of energy relate to the prospect of making money? It's worth considering that setting up a business may require a long period of sustained research, where skills are acquired and customers found, before any income is generated at all.

Some questions to think about

● If you are a student or starting a business, have you worked out how many days per year there are available to run your business?

● Have you calculated the time involved in making a product or delivering a service appropriately, in seconds, minutes, hours or days?

● If you are managing a business, how many business days in relation to numbers of employees do you currently have? Do you have 220 days per annum (sole enterprise), 440 days (joint enterprise), 2,200 days (micro-enterprise) or what?

To make a profit, products have to be made or services delivered in the minimal amount of time at the least expense, and sold at the right time for the best price, in the quantities desired. It's worth remembering, just being skilled or having a stock of products unfortunately does not guarantee sales if there is no market demand.

Valuing time

Procrastination is the thief of time.

Edward Young, poet and playwright, 1683–1765

Using time efficiently by improving the use of it can make the difference between winning or losing contracts, meeting or missing deadlines, maximizing profits or suffering losses. It is very easy to lose months of business time over a year, drained away by distractions or inefficient use of the time you have. We will explore this topic further in the 'Enterprise skills booster', at the end of this chapter.

Time in relation to money

Costing and pricing is a large, complex subject, especially if you are not particularly good at mathematics, so let's first understand the fundamental principles. It is an easy mistake to undervalue the time. Entrepreneurs often fail to factor into calculations leisure time and business activity that in itself does not directly generate income.

Initial points

Many business owners cost time for themselves or employees the basis of 220, 200 or 177 days of the year; others may cost on 100, 50 or fewer. How so, you may ask?

Before explaining further, a few phrases need clarifying:

- The word 'leisure' can mean any non-business activity: resting, socializing, household chores, childcare, shopping, DIY, gardening, moving house, entertainment, hobbies, keeping fit, holidays and so on.

- Not everyone takes 'weekends' off, but you may well take a day, and other time off during the week, equating to a similar amount of time. It is foolish to overwork, and if you do, overall productivity will slow down.

- You may argue you are never ill, but it is likely you may have to care for others who are poorly during a year, perhaps children or relatives. Alternatively, you may store illness up, and have a bumper year of misery, losing a few weeks or months of productivity at some point in the future.

- Everyone needs at least four weeks off a year; work to live, not live to work!

There are…
365 days in a year. Working five days a week, there are 52 weekends equating to 104 days of leisure.
$365 - 104 = 261$ days

Over the year there are eight bank holidays, usually for leisure unless you decide to work them.
$261 - 8 = 253$ days

On top of this we will allow 25 days of leisure as holiday time.
$253 - 25 = 228$ days

Let's allow between six and eight sick days, or days spent looking after poorly children or relatives.
$228 - 8 = 220$ days of business or employment time.

The business cake theory

Nothing is a waste of time if you use the experience wisely.

Auguste Rodin, sculptor, 1840–1917

Business and leisure time

Figure 8.2 summarizes more or less the way time works out. You may argue all you wish about the amount of time spent working. **What we are trying to understand is the number of days you have to run a business and generate money.**

If you are an employee, the employer pays you by the hour, day or week. That wage has to cover the days you work and all the days you are not working. In the same way, when you start a business, consider that that profits made on productive days have to support other business or leisure activities that do not produce income.

Other expenses

There will be other expenses to calculate when working out service fees or pricing products, especially if you are making large investment into equipment or renting premises.

Business and part-time work

When starting a business, it may not be realistic to assume you will be able to find enough paid opportunities to earn a regular income, five days a week for about 47 weeks of the year. There will be days or even months you have no work at all, while during others you may have a flow of offers. It is important to work out living and business expenses in relation to the amount of days that achieve profitable output. This is why getting

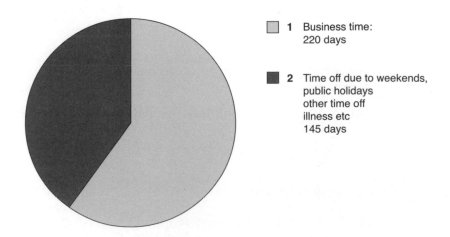

1 Business time:
   220 days

2 Time off due to weekends,
   public holidays
   other time off
   illness etc
   145 days

Figure 8.2 The business cake theory: business and leisure time

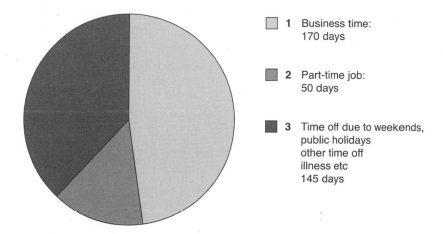

1   Business time:
    170 days

2   Part-time job:
    50 days

3   Time off due to weekends,
    public holidays
    other time off
    illness etc
    145 days

Figure 8.3 Business time in relation to leisure and employment time

a part-time job, presented in Figure 8.3 as 50 days, can be useful in the early months or years to support yourself while getting a venture off the ground. However, as you will see it cuts down the time you can dedicate to your business. The business time of 170 days featured in Figure 8.3, may not be wholly dedicated to earning money, as we will discover later (Figures 8.4, 8.5 and 8.6).

It's essential to calculate the cost-effectiveness of production or delivery. If you have a sole enterprise, you might be able to manufacture or deliver 10 products or services a day, or only one. **Realistic costing has to be applied to capacity, in relation to time and costs**. As well as considering this, you also have to factor in the time that it takes to sell to customers. It may take hardly any time to make a sale if the customer purchases from a shop or your website. However, much more time and effort may be required to make a sale, for instance if you are selling by phone, sending out promotional materials or making a presentation. It could take even longer if it involves negotiation and tendering for work, taking many days or weeks!

Leaving simplicity behind

Time can become difficult to cost the more complex a business becomes. It is worth bearing in mind that greater amounts of profit can be more easily accumulated if you can make money without personally having to spend physical time and effort earning it. Good examples of labour-saving initiatives are making money without further effort in the form of earning royalties by licensing artistic works, designs, brands or patents. Investing in hiring hi-tech machines to prototype products and manufacture in large quantities will save a great deal of time. Employing assistants, or even a manager to take over your role, will free up your time so you can expand the business further.

Understanding business time

As you can see from Figure 8.4 business time is spent in different ways. Your annual business time represented in the pie chart (no pun intended) may cover 220, 200, 170 or 100 days of the year. It is possible it covers 365 days, in the case of a large well-staffed enterprise functioning 24 hours a day. However, let's not complicate matters at this stage but simply analyse the basic activities that are involved in running any kind of business, whether a self-employed electrician or a global utilities company.

The ideas embodied in the 'business cake theory' are based upon Japanese business philosophy. Figure 8.4 describes different business activities. As you

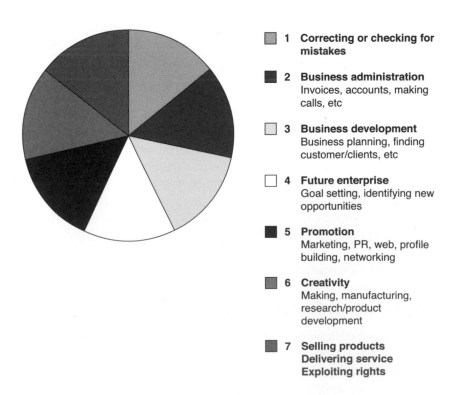

1　**Correcting or checking for mistakes**

2　**Business administration**
Invoices, accounts, making calls, etc

3　**Business development**
Business planning, finding customer/clients, etc

4　**Future enterprise**
Goal setting, identifying new opportunities

5　**Promotion**
Marketing, PR, web, profile building, networking

6　**Creativity**
Making, manufacturing, research/product development

7　**Selling products Delivering service Exploiting rights**

Figure 8.4 Business cake theory: your business time

will understand, it is fundamental to maximize the amount of time associated with point 7 in the list below, 'Selling and delivering' the service: that is, the actual number of days that income is generated.

Seven segments of business time

But at my back I always hear Time's winged chariot drawing near.

Andrew Marvell, poet, 1621–1678

1. Correcting and checking for mistakes

This is a vital task. If mistakes are spotted then further time and money will not be wasted. When running any type of enterprise it is important to double-check your own work, and that of others.

2. Business administration

For the average small business this can take up an enormous amount of time. Even as a sole enterprise, allowing one whole day per week for administration is not unrealistic; this includes bookkeeping, invoicing, responding to e-mails and so on. Larger companies invest heavily in computerized systems and management software to cut down time being spent on manual processing.

3. Business development

Business planning and cultivating customers in the early stages of an enterprise or during a major growth period can take weeks and months. As with all business planning activity, not all of the time invested will yield results. However, without an action plan there will no focus or strategy.

4. Future enterprise

To run a successful business it's essential to seek out opportunities several months or years down the line. To meet future objectives it is important to start as early a possible, for instance booking for trade fairs 12 to 24 months away.

5. Promotion

Marketing, networking, developing promotional materials and websites take a great deal of effort, even after putting time and money into promotion. Making mistakes in the early years are common, such as missing important copy deadlines for magazines, or poorly conceived branding.

What is essential is to learn valuable lessons from mistakes and avoid repeating them.

6. Creativity

Exploring product development, research, prototyping, experimenting and manufacture of your product or refining a service are also of supreme importance.

7. Selling and delivering

This point is fundamental. You need to maximize profit-generating time. Even for a large firm functioning 24/7, the emphasis for money generation will be weighted directly or indirectly on certain activities or individuals.

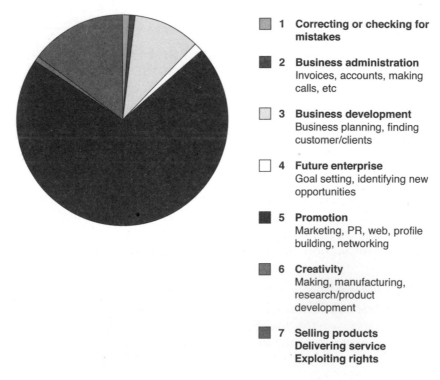

1   **Correcting or checking for mistakes**

2   **Business administration**
    Invoices, accounts, making calls, etc

3   **Business development**
    Business planning, finding customer/clients

4   **Future enterprise**
    Goal setting, identifying new opportunities

5   **Promotion**
    Marketing, PR, web, profile building, networking

6   **Creativity**
    Making, manufacturing, research/product development

7   **Selling products**
    Delivering service
    Exploiting rights

Figure 8.5 Business cake theory: how business start-up time is used

How business start-up time is used

A common problem in start-ups, whether sole or team-enterprises, is the amount of time that has to be allocated to planning and marketing. The proportions shown in Figure 8.5 should prepare you for the fact that about 70 per cent of the first year may have to be dedicated to investing money and time into promotion. It is likely that little income will be generated during the first few months or years. Many businesses that take out loans during the start-up period will not fully pay them back until several years latter.

Money-making time

It is important to maximize money-making time (Figure 8.6), when making sales of products or delivering services. Some freelancers for instance will only obtain paid work on 177 days of the year if they are lucky. They may be fortunate that the other six factors involved in running their sole enterprise take only 43 days. The money earned on 177 days, will need to cover 43 days of other business activities and 145 days of leisure time.

If you are making products or delivering a service that cannot be exploited by licensing and receiving repeat payments in the form of royal-

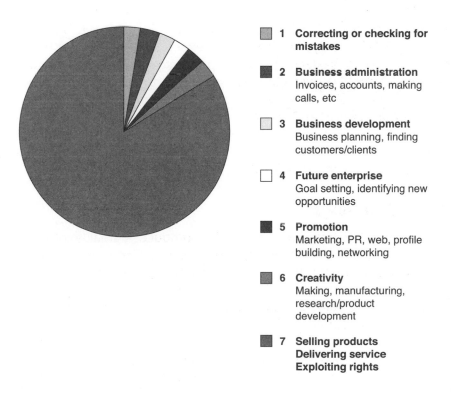

1 **Correcting or checking for mistakes**

2 **Business administration**
Invoices, accounts, making calls, etc

3 **Business development**
Business planning, finding customers/clients

4 **Future enterprise**
Goal setting, identifying new opportunities

5 **Promotion**
Marketing, PR, web, profile building, networking

6 **Creativity**
Making, manufacturing, research/product development

7 **Selling products
Delivering service
Exploiting rights**

Figure 8.6 Money-making time

ties, then there is a limit to how much money you can make per year. Income relates to the number of products or services that not only can be made or delivered, but also can be sold by the sole or team-enterprise, or employees. This is why it is important to cost your own hourly rate or that of employees carefully, based upon level of expertise or experience. There is no point employing someone as cheaply as you can, if that person doesn't have the skills to achieve targets. It is better to pay more money for higher calibre individuals who will make a difference.

Service business

It can be impossible for most sole enterprises that are tied to a daily rate to turn over more than £30,000 to £35,000 per year. The reason is that if, for instance, the trader gains 150 days of paid work at £200 per day that makes an income of £30,000 per annum. After income tax and the running costs of the business are taken into consideration, the tender may have to live on £20,000 or less.

Product business

When selling products, in simplistic terms, if the sales price is £30 and the item costs £6.50 to make, including other expenses, a fledgling entrepreneur would have to make and sell 1,000 products at £30 each per year to generate £30,000 income. After paying income tax and other business expenses, that would leave the entrepreneur about £20,000 per year from the profits to live on. Therefore, a trader who had a market stall for two days a week for 50 weeks of the year (100 days of selling time) would have to sell 10 products at £30 each day to make £600 a week (which yields £30,000 income per annum).

Wholesale business

Consider a business that makes and sells a product. A small joint enterprise, say a husband and wife team, might sell goods from their website, but key orders are from retailers that are placed during trade fairs, which may only happen over a few days three or four times a year. Therefore, the opportunity to gain substantial orders of many tens of thousands of pounds may only happen on 20 days over a year.

Costing and pricing is a great deal more complicated than these examples suggest, but they will be sufficient for you to grasp the general principle.

Notes for managers

Managers must be aware it is likely they will be able to obtain between 200–225 days of work from the average full-time employee. If you pay employees £25,000 per year, then they must ideally generate £75,000 a year, or at least £50,000 in real financial value, to make it worthwhile employing them. Their input must sufficiently contribute to the profitability of the business.

Closing thoughts

Do not try to do it all.

William Julian King, engineering professor and author, 1902–1983

Is this business running you, or are you running this business?

A crucial enterprise skill is understanding time in relation to all the numerous business expenses, including capacity, in terms of what you or an employee can achieve, so that goals can be achieved. What is worth bearing in mind is that there is never enough time in the day or week to get through the number of tasks that may face you.

As a business owner one must apply some judgement and common sense to the situation. Work will always be there, it continually flows in like the sea. Extending the working week into weekends or taking paperwork on holiday, as mentioned earlier in Chapter 4, 'How to focus', will only decrease the quality of output and make mistakes more likely.

Key points

- Analyse your week, and calculate how much time you waste, eg watching junk TV, leisure software, writing long e-mails.
- Think through how you could use an extra eight hours a week, created by giving up watching TV on weekday evenings, or other time-saving initiatives.
- Work out how you can maximize productivity time in the week, though bringing in time-saving systems.
- Invest in quality leisure time, eg for rest, socializing, keeping fit.
- Look at a year planner and count how many business days you have available. If you are in full-time employment, realistically at a stretch you may have 50 to 75 days over a year to dedicate to running a hobby or lifestyle business. If you are in part-time work, you might find you have 50 to 170 days of business time. If a start-up or a

manager, then it's likely there will be about 220 days. If a manager in a large firm, the business may well operate everyday, but you won't!

● Calculate what your personal financial needs for the year are, add on business start-up costs and estimated running costs. Then you can work out rough targets in terms of a number of days worked or products sold. Remember costing time is a bit more complicated than this, but this is a good starting point.

Enterprise skills booster

Use the tables below to help you think about time saving and wasting activities. The tables are partially complete, so you can put in your own suggestions.

The idea is to help you minimize waste of time and introduce time-saving systems.

Table 8.1   Time wasters

Junk TV	Leisure software	Trying to find things you have lost	Untidiness
Queuing	Traffic jams	Getting lost	Being late
Writing long e-mails	Hangovers	Draining people	

Table 8.2   Time savers

Sometimes using the telephone	Being tidy	Automated systems	Colour-coded files
Keeping e-mails short	Delegating work or sharing tasks	Conducting meetings by phone/web	Early nights and early starts
Being on time	Seeking expert advice	Backing up computer systems	

- Decide how to create more time in the week to help you focus on your business.
- Start drafting out what you will start to do, and what you have to stop doing!
  - What difference do you hope these changes make?
- Be prepared to dedicate time to setting up systems such as colour coding files, using symbols, coloured card or Post-it notes.
- Prioritize what systems you would like to improve.
  - How will you achieve this?
  - Will you do it yourself? Hire in help? Delegate?
  - Set some deadlines to complete these tasks.

Complex procedures, as mentioned in the previous chapter's 'Key Points', can be grouped into key themes or stages. They can be made more immediately accessible to employees by having instructions written on A5 coloured cards, and placed in small see-through index boxes in each office. This will make it easy for new staff to refer to the cards without having to needlessly interrupt other staff or spend time trying to unearth guidance on the firm's intranet.

9

Legal and ethical matters

Laws are like spider webs through which the big flies pass and the little ones get caught.

Honoré de Balzac, novelist and poet, 1799–1850

Compliance with the laws that govern business ensures that a business trades legitimately. Everyone is aware of companies operating in 'black market' conditions that are usually not officially registered, contravene regulations and are most likely uninsured. It is essential you do not join their ranks.

Before starting a business, you should learn as much as possible about the relevant legislation governing your industry sector. The difficulty of this task must not be underestimated. Failure to understand what to do may trigger some form of litigation. Bear in mind, ignorance is no defence where the law is concerned.

It is quite possible that during the course of setting up or expanding a business, some contravening of regulations could inadvertently occur. This can be due to simple unawareness of obscure legislation, or a decision to bend the law slightly because complying with all legislation in the early days is thought to be too costly. Speak with any proprietor and they will recall times when they have 'stretched the elastic' and managed to get away with small misdemeanours. For those who failed to realize this was not a sensible way to continue, stories will be recounted, of 'getting caught out', fined or even imprisoned.

The procrastinator

A professional artist who had been running a small creative business for many years was unexpectedly offered several large commissions. The artist did not know much about business, so decided to seek advice.

The adviser suggested that he should invest in having proper terms and conditions drawn up, as the risks and liabilities concerned with his business activities had increased dramatically. Among other things, he needed to include a clause in the contract about cancellation fees. If a commission was cancelled after the contract had been agreed and signed, the artist would still be entitled to 25 per cent of the original fee.

Six months later the adviser met with the artist again and unfortunately he had not yet acted on her advice. Due to the artist's procrastination or reluctance to invest in terms of trade he had already lost out – a commission for £40,000 had been cancelled after the contract had been signed, and without an agreed cancellation fee he was left with nothing. If he had taken the advice given he could have gained £10,000.

Act immediately upon guidance from business advisers, accountants or solicitors. Failure to do so can have serious consequences for your business.

A man who is his own lawyer has a fool for a client.

Old American proverb, Philadelphia, 1809

The impact of law varies dramatically from country to country. In the UK it is continually being amended by Acts of Parliament, case law and EU Directives.

It is essential to grasp the rudiments of how the law applies to your business and acquire sufficient knowledge to implement it. When laws and regulations change, they can directly affect your business. The smoking ban in the early years of the 21st century and bylaws preventing cars parking in town centres, for instance, have caused many clubs and shops to close.

Don't be your 'own lawyer' – obtain proper guidance. It is advisable to form a relationship with a local firm of solicitors. Seeking the services of a professional adviser will help you cope with unexpected problems and keep you updated about your rights and obligations. Ideally, find a solicitor who understands your industry, eg retail, manufacture, financial services, health, arts, catering, etc.

Don't get caught out. Legal problems almost always arise from poor communication.

Mike Southon and Chris West, 1953–/1954–, authors of *The Beermat Entrepreneur* and other books

Failure to seek professional advice when experiencing some kind of legal problem is another common error for entrepreneurs and managers. It is likely that you will be unable to sort all matters out yourself. **Always seek advice before making an accusation or responding to any made**. Equally, you may receive an e-mail or phone call accusing you of unlawful activity. It is best not to say anything until you have sought advice.

Dealing with allegations

You may need advice on how to initiate an allegation or respond to one. A solicitor will advise you on how to communicate in such circumstances, and act on your behalf. When in difficulties, it is easy to make mistakes in the way we conduct ourselves. This could be because we are angry, upset or possibly not aware of all the facts. You may be accused of anything: it might be products or services causing harm, such as poisoning or injuring customers; or that you have stolen data, goods or equipment from clients, or illegally copied a competitor's products or branding.

Choose your battles

When deceitful people are alerted to the fact they have been 'caught out', then, depending on the severity of situation, they may issue a denial, become silent or even disappear. This can subsequently preclude seeking a just resolution. The assistance of a solicitor can prevent minor matters escalating into exhausting conflict. It may be a more serious matter, possibly for the attention of the authorities, including the police. It is wise to seek counsel with a legal expert before taking action.

Litigation will distract you from running a business, and in most cases the time and cost involved do not justify the meagre rewards of such battles. Some small businesses never recover from such experiences and cease trading.

Crime

It is a three-pipe problem, and I beg that you won't speak to me for 50 minutes.

'Sherlock Holmes', fictional detective created by Sir Arthur Conan Doyle, novelist, 1859–1930

It is likely that over the years your business will be the target of crime in one form or another.

It is essential to have an emergency plan (aka disaster recovery planning) for your business. To begin this process, undertake risk assessments as described in Chapter 2, 'Understanding risk'. This will help you develop control measures and a business recovery plan, for instance not storing all stock in one warehouse, taking out insurance, investing in security measures and back-up systems, protecting designs and trademarks by registration.

UK readers may be interested to read more about the effects of crime on small businesses and insurance issues on the Federation of Small Businesses' website, www.fsb.org.uk. For those in the United States, The National Association for the Self-employed, www.nase.org, similarly provides surveys and reports on US business matters.

Ethics

Once you get rid of integrity the rest is a piece of cake.

Larry Hagman, actor, 1931–, recalling his favourite J R Ewing line from the
TV show *Dallas*

Developing trust in the business world is vital. Damage done to your reputation can have catastrophic consequences.

There is increasing public awareness of ethical issues. Consumers are becoming more selective about how they spend or invest their money. There are numerous issues that feature in the media, including exploitation, pollution and waste. Fair trade, ecology and global warming are now important ethical concerns. Making poor decisions, for instance about how you dispose of toxic waste, can destroy trust in your business and may result in prosecution.

More carrot

Many business leaders and managers are seizing the initiative by setting their own professional standards, including corporate social responsibility initiatives. In the last few years, new entrepreneurs have become conscious that they should adopt an 'ethical or environmental' policy. You only have to look on the internet for evidence of good practice concerning ethical sourcing of supplies, reducing carbon emissions and conserving resources.

Good case studies include the large-scale initiative of redeveloping wasteland for the London Olympics. The Olympic Delivery Authority is adopting a strict regime of recycling. Any useful materials found on the site, such as stone, metal and bitumen, are re-used in construction. However, this is mainly a publicly funded initiative, and at the time of writing the credibility of the project is in jeopardy due to spiralling costs.

IKEA® is currently an excellent example of modern corporate responsibility. The company donates money to local community projects and is actively involved in supporting UNICEF and environmental initiatives.

Whether you are a small or large enterprise, demonstrating social and ecological concern is not simply a public relations exercise; it is about maintaining values and building trust with customers and suppliers.

More stick

Trading standards laws, and new environmental and planning regulations, combined with a change in consumers' attitudes to ethical matters, are compelling companies to rethink their relationships with suppliers and the local community. For instance in many real estate proposals, provision of affordable housing and resources for the community is included to improve the likelihood of gaining planning permission.

At the time of writing, many entrepreneurs I have met are unaware of packaging regulations and CE marking of their products. It is worth realizing that flouting environment protection laws can result in substantial fines.

UK readers seeking information about environmental regulations should visit the Department for Food and Rural Affairs' website, www.defra.gov.uk, or the Department for Business, Enterprise & Regulatory Reform, www.berr.gov.uk. If based in the United States, contact the US Environmental Protection Agency, www.epa.gov.

Trust

If we are not trusted, we have no business.

Larry Page, co-founder of Google™, 1973–

When companies abuse the trust of suppliers and customers through bad practice, the public will vote with their feet. Building trust in a brand with consumers or with business associates takes a considerable amount of time. It is very easy to undo such work in an instant. Trust is developed in many ways, including complying with the law, trading safely and being properly insured.

It is very important to consider your own ethical values and those of the businesses with which you trade. To maintain your standards you have to be careful. If you find businesses are behaving in an objectionable way, it may be wise to distance yourself from them. This will reduce the risk of damage to your own credibility in the future.

It's worth preparing for a breakdown of trust, such as a broken promise or breach of contract. As part of assessing risk, you have to be able to deal with the consequences.

If you would like to study the subject of business ethics in more detail, I suggest reading, *Your Ethical Business: How to plan, start and succeed in a company with a conscience* (2007), by Paul Allen.

Risks and insurance

Insurance! Insurance! How boring! But what-do-ya-know somebody has an accident and suddenly it gets very interesting.

Mr Mouse, catchphrase, esure® Advertising campaign, 2005–

We live in an increasingly litigious society, thanks to the transatlantic influence of US ambulance-chasing lawyers coming here. The enthusiasm to sue is taking precedence over the acceptance of personal responsibility. The 'blame culture' is causing liability insurance costs to spiral. Expensive premiums increase the overheads of micro-businesses to such an extent that some just give up and close.

Unfortunately, there are unscrupulous traders that do operate without adequate insurance cover for all their business activities. Certain types of insurance are required by law, such as public liability for business premises that are open to visitors, customers, or house employees. If you employ people, even if it is just a part-time assistant (paid on a payroll system not as freelancers), then you will require employers' liability insurance.

Other insurances are not statutory requirements but are simply a sensible precaution – insuring equipment against fire, flood and theft. It is wise when self-employed (also termed working freelance), to take out public liability insurance to cover your own liability against risks such as causing injury or damage to people or equipment when working for clients at their premises, or at other locations.

In the lifetime of a business, it is highly likely you will make a few mistakes. This may result in an exaggerated claim for compensation made against you. **To minimize this risk, it is vital that you have written terms and conditions, which you send to clients with order forms or service agreements**. This will reduce your liability to events outside your control.

When you take out an insurance policy, read it carefully and clarify exactly what is covered. Whenever venturing into new areas of business, one must assess the risks, in order to minimize or manage them. Remember that insurance companies base their quotation on the unlikelihood of damage or injury being caused, whereas, the applicant takes out insurance based upon the likelihood of loss or harm happening.

When taking out insurance cover, always ask about 'all risks' policies or 'package' deals that can cover a number of liabilities including legal expenses insurance. Always be truthful when dealing with insurance companies; make full disclosure about your business activities and premises.

UK readers may be interested to learn more about advisable or statutory insurance cover from the British Insurers Brokers' Association's website, www.biba.org.uk, or Business Link, www.businesslink.gov.uk. Those in the United States may wish to view their own government business information site, www.business.gov. (These websites also have up-to-date articles and free fact sheets on different laws and trading regulations.)

Intellectual and industrial property

Intellectual property is the oil of the 21st century.

Mark Getty, Chairman Getty Images®, 1960–

What is intellectual property?

Intellectual property (IP) is a collection of legal and financial rights concerning 'artistic' copyright, design right, trademarks and patents. Some countries classify the latter three as 'industrial property'.

Intellectual property law governs the ownership and exploitation of rights by 'authors' such as artists, designers, business owners or inventors. This area of law is fiendishly complicated to understand. Before your business can make money from licensing or reproducing artwork, products, brands and industrial solutions, you must understand how the law applies in your own country and any with which you seek to trade. Even after a great deal of study, it may be best to seek the advice about commercially sensitive ideas with a solicitor specializing in IP or a patent agent.

We currently have no single global intellectual property law. However, it is highly likely that by the end of the 21st century this will seem to be a surprising historical fact. Many countries have agreed to recognize each other's IP laws – some treaties go back many years. The European Union has made a start in harmonizing laws governing trademarks (business names and brands) and design rights (drawings or products which usually have a function, such as sit on it, wear it, illuminate a room, etc). At the time of writing, the Europe Patent Office is exploring how to unify patent law across all member states.

Whether you are a student, an entrepreneur or a manager, there will be a number of intellectual property issues to consider. A list of useful websites is included at the end of this section. Meanwhile here is a short outline.

Copyright

Artistic works created by authors, musicians, writers (including software), artists, film makers and photographers usually fall under the protection of copyright. This is an automatic right and requires no registration, although the idea has to be expressed in some form and must be original – a drawing, a recording, photograph, script, model or the like.

However, for US citizens there are other benefits in registering artistic works with the US Copyright Office. In the United States copyright protection lasts the lifetime of the author and, as a general rule, 75 years after their death. In the UK it is 70 years (note that some art forms have shorter spans of protection).

When artworks are literally copied, it constitutes an 'infringement'. When ideas embodied in a work are stolen from others and used without academic acknowledgement or permission, this is often referred to as 'plagiarism'. When products are reproduced illegally, this is defined as 'counterfeiting' or 'piracy'.

If you believe your artistic works, branded goods or products are being reproduced without your permission, then obtain advice from an IP solicitor quickly. It may be worth pursuing the 'copyists' in or out of court, under civil or criminal laws. However, to gain any advantage you have to act swiftly and not procrastinate.

Copyright laws change periodically, and so does the length of protection. So with all matters of law, seek appropriate professional advice.

Design right

This part of IP law refers to the applied arts, in the field of craft and design. Usually design right covers a multitude of three-dimensional products, such as chairs, lighting, ceramics, clothing and jewellery (in the United States it is referred to as design patent). It also covers textiles and patterned material. This is where copyright crosses over into design. If an artwork such as an illustration of a flower is reproduced as a pattern and printed on fabric, it can be registered under design right.

In the UK there are special rules governing this right. You have to register drawings or photographs of the products with the Intellectual Property Office within a year of making them or from first public disclosure. If protection is sought in the United States, designs are registered at the US Patent and Trademark Office. Once again, regulations and length of protection vary. In the UK it is 25 years and in the United States it is 14 years from the date of registration. This registered right varies from country to country. It's worth realizing that 'unregistered' rights also have a period of recognition.

Business or brand names

A website domain name **is not the same a**s a registered trademark. Having a business name that a sole trader or partnership is trading under **is not the same as** registering a company name. Holding the rights to your business or company name **is not the same as** registration and owning a trademark.

If you are able to register a brand or business name with the Intellectual Property Office on the Trademark Register – or if you are trading in the United States at the United States Patent and Trademark Office – then you alone can exploit that name in the given territory (with certain limited exceptions). In the UK a trademark has to be renewed every 10 years to retain protection. The US system is slightly different, with new registrations having the first renewal date upon five years from registration, then every 10 years.

However, if you fail to register a business name or it is rejected, you may still be able to use it (again with certain limitations), and the laws of 'infringement' and 'passing off' will apply under 'copyright' law. US trademark law is far more encompassing, even protecting areas of artistic style. Such issues are not included in British trademark law.

Patent

Inventions are legally protected by the granting of a patent. The idea has to be innovative and have an industrial application. It could exist as a drawing or as a functioning prototype. **If you have invented a machine, mechanism, device or material, do not reveal it to anyone or disclose it publicly**. If you have the expertise and patience to search through the patent listings and are confident there is nothing matching your idea, make an appointment with a patent agent or IP solicitor. You can pay for patent searches, and there may be some other legal expenses involved, before filing a patent application.

If you are seeking protection in the UK, patents require registering at the Intellectual Property Office, while if seeking protection in United States registration is at the US Patent and Trademark Office. In both countries, protection lasts for 20 years. The procedures are not straightforward and you will benefit from specialist advice.

Some thoughts...

It is worth being aware of 'patent-busting' tactics. Many firms invest resources in circumventing inventors' and other firms' licensing rights. It is also important to consider the wisdom of embarking on patent registration, if for instance, the pace of innovation is likely to supersede your invention or the product is not commercially viable. When approaching any manufacturer or investor after you have filed your patent application, it is still advisable to treat your working knowledge as a trade secret, and make use of non-disclosure agreements (NDAs).

Useful resources

Contact the Intellectual Property and Industrial Property/Patent Offices that govern your own country; most provide free downloadable guides:

● www.ipo.gov.uk: Intellectual Property Office for UK citizens and those seeking protection in the UK. This government website covers all aspects of IP.

- http://oami.europa.eu: Official Harmonization in the Internal Market, the European Agency responsible for EU Trademark and Design Right registration.
- www.copyright.gov: United States Copyright Office, The Library of Congress, for registration of copyright for US citizens.
- www.uspto.gov: US Patent and Trademark Office, for protection in the United States, covering patents, design patent and trademark registration.

Contracts

Laws, like houses, lean in on another.

Edmund Burke, statesman and philosopher, 1729–1797

Contracts can be oral or written. They consist of four elements: an 'offer', 'acceptance', 'consideration' and intent to form 'legal relations'. 'Consideration' refers to something given in exchange. This is usually money, but it could be access to resources, material goods or equipment.

It is good practice to confirm spoken agreements concerning legal or financial liabilities and intellectual property matters in writing. This could be in the form of a letter of agreement or a traditional contract. There are many types of contracts. For a business owner it is advisable to have them drawn up by a suitably qualified solicitor or lawyer. Contracts include: terms and conditions, copyright licence, letters engaging a free-lancer, employee contracts and order forms, to name but a few.

Contract law and licensing of intellectual rights are particularly complex business subjects. If you do not possess an analytical mind, then it is beneficial to join a trade or professional body to gain advice or hire the services of legal experts. It can be the case, for instance, that in a 15-page contract there may be only a few words that require deletion, replacement or alteration. The difficulty lies in knowing precisely which clauses to amend, and how. Legalese is like the language of finance, and without a thorough understanding, you may agree to an unsatisfactory deal.

Never begin work on a project or send goods to third parties until a contract has been agreed and signed. If you start work or send goods away before signing a contract, it means you accept the offer. It may be unwise to do so as the written contract may be different from the initial verbal agreement.

When reading a contract always check which country it is governed by, whether for instance it is under the law of England and Wales, or Scottish or US law. If it isn't mentioned, contact a solicitor for legal advice.

Other important laws

Trading legally

There are numerous restrictions (and consumer watchdogs) governing the advertising of products and services, their manufacture, presentation and delivery to the customer. Seek advice from your local enterprise agency, or contact government departments directly to request literature.

Employment law

Regulation and the rights of employees have strengthened over the last decade, directed towards ending discrimination and improving conditions of employment for all. Business owners don't set out with the intention of marrying all their employees. However, the number of promises an employer has to undertake when taking on a new member of staff is tantamount to a blanket proposal.

To sack difficult or lazy workers is becoming more difficult, given the degree of proof required of wrongdoing and the risk that the worker will contest it. You can still sack people, but doing so is not as easy as it once was.

Managing the process

It is desirable when first taking on employees to invest in a manual explaining all the regulations, such as Barry Cushway's *The Employer's Handbook* (2008). Larger firms can rely on their own human resource departments and welfare staff to take on this responsibility. When you are expanding a sole enterprise it may well be worth seeking guidance from a freelance HR consultant or specialist employment lawyer when searching for your first employees. They will be able to advise you on recruitment, interviewing and management of staff. When disputes arise between yourself and staff, it can be useful to hire HR consultants or lawyers for short periods to mediate in difficult circumstances. Your accountant will also be able to advise you on the technicalities of setting up a payroll system.

Health and safety

The law pertaining to heath and safety seeks to reduce the risk of harm and death being caused in the workplace. It covers every variety of activity: use of equipment, storage, signage, hazardous substances, fire safety and the construction of premises.

Many laws relating to safety translate as basic common sense. Unfortunately, we live in a world where people lack this, or will unjustly blame others for any injuries caused. For that reason, and not simply from concern for safety, you should make yourself familiar with this area of the law.

The perils of ignoring compliance with regulations

I recall an incident from earlier this decade, when two young entrepreneurs were highlighted on a regional news programme. They had taken over a derelict building and planned to hold an illegal party. The landlord of the building in which they had temporarily squatted, and the local council, pleaded with them not to go ahead with the venture. The maverick duo were interviewed on the television: they were enthusiastic and saw the escapade as a bit of fun.

I thought to myself, as a former teacher of health and safety, that there was a great deal to consider, quite apart from the expense of making venues safe for large numbers of people. There was a lot of legal regulation with which to comply. I did not think these two young people fully understood what they were taking on.

The next day, it was reported on the news that a young man had tragically died at the event and part of the building had been destroyed by fire.

UK readers seeking guidance about the regulations should visit the Health and Safety Executive, www.hse.gov.uk. For those in the United States, contact the US Department of Labor, Occupational Safety and Health Administrator, www.osha.gov.

General points

When running a business it is sensible to bear in mind some basic rules:

- Never work if you or your team are tired. The likelihood is that poor decisions will be made, and that the chances of injury will be increased.
- Make sure when hiring employees that they are competent. Incompetent workers are a liability, and will place undue pressure on other employees.

● Double-check references, and request at least one professional referee who has known the applicant for a minimum of four years.

● To avoid being burdened in the long term with the worse than useless, always include a probationary period in any employment contract.

Building and planning regulations

Once a business breaks out of a bedroom into an office, studio, workshop or retail premises, costs can suddenly escalate. Listening to US business leaders over the years, it appears that running a business in the United States is easier and less expensive than in the UK.

Whenever a business wishes to alter the use of a building or build new premises, it is advisable to seek the advice of architects, surveyors, solicitors, building contractors, building inspectors, local council officials, planning officers and health and safety reps, and organize a visit by the fire brigade. Just to name a few! It's easier to find suitable premises that will require no change of use and little alteration to suit your purposes.

UK readers seeking guidance about planning permission and building regulations should contact the Royal Institute of Chartered Surveyors, www.rics.org, and the Planning Portal, www.planningportal.com. Those based in the United States should contact the US Department of Labor, www.dol.gov.

Tax

He is spending a year dead for tax reasons.

Douglas Adams, novelist, 1952–2001

For many years after his death, Freddie Mercury, the lead singer of Queen, continued to receive a salary. This came to public attention, and the band's accountant explained that the payments were made for 'tax reasons'. This is one of the bizarre stories arising from the baffling number of regulations concerning income, corporation and value added tax.

It is important to understand the basics of taxation, in order to minimize and structure tax payments. Payments to the Revenue can be due many months or years after the end of the original accounting period. Failure to provide for future tax payments can easily create a cash flow problem or, worse still, insolvency. **Avoid borrowing money to pay tax, as this will set off a never-ending cycle of debt**.

At the outset you may decide to do your own books and annual returns. As an enterprise grows, it can become difficult to find enough time to do it yourself. Engage the services of a qualified accountant. In Britain there is an old saying, 'a good accountant will always find their fee'. Why pay excessive tax bills when you don't have to? An accountant will be able to advise you about accountancy software, and should save you much time and money. These can then be spent in ways that are more fruitful.

UK readers seeking guidance about tax and business registration should visit HM Revenue & Customs' website, www.hmrc.gov.uk, or Companies House, www.companieshouse.gov.uk. If you are based in the United States, contact the Internal Revenue Service, www.irs.gov.

To find a qualified accountant, view a list of registered 'certified' or 'chartered' accountants at www.accaglobal.com or www.icaew.co.uk.

Closing thoughts

In civilized life, law floats in a sea of ethics.

Earl Warren, US Chief Justice, 1891–1974

Try not to underestimate how complicated laws pertaining to business are. It is easy to fall foul of regulations because there are so many of them. There are people trading today who simply do not understand the basic rules governing their industry. It is vital that you do not run your business upon 'a wing and a prayer' basis. Make sure you find a simple and effective method of keeping informed about legal issues; this could be through regular advice sessions or reading business newsletters about developments in your field.

Key points

- Set out to learn as much as you can about legal issues. Avoid reliance on the internet, unless viewing information from trusted sources, such as government web pages, up-to-date articles on accountants or solicitors' websites.
- Go to talks by legal experts and read guides to the law published by reputable imprints or professional bodies. Always double-check anything you have found out from a book or the web, as the law may have changed recently.

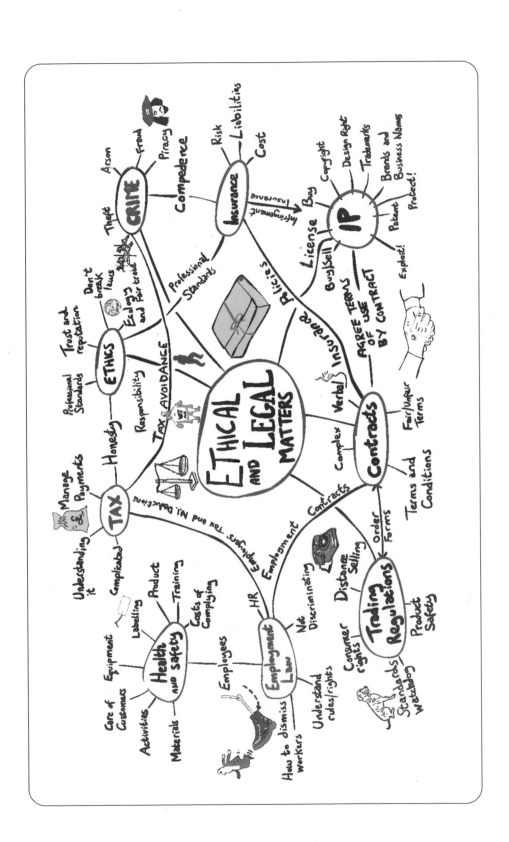

- Develop an enquiring mindset. To make best use of an adviser's time, list as many questions as possible you don't have answers to.

- Health-check your business by re-analysing all current insurance policies against current or future plans. Re-read all those terms and conditions and other contracts that are frequently doled out without a second thought.

- If you are unhappy or suspicious about a situation, print out copies of e-mails and written correspondence. Keep a daily diary, with times and dates of conversations or telephone calls. Such evidence is vital when trying to prove innocence or wrongdoing sometimes months or many years later.

- Look at what contracts you need to have drawn up to operate your business professionally. Avoid pinching and cribbing other businesses' terms and conditions from websites. This is an amateur approach and may land you in hot water. Use them as a guide, but invest properly in having contracts drawn up by specialists.

Enterprise skills booster

- List a few legal problems or situations you are facing or likely to face. (If you struggle to think of any, then you need to do research into regulations and laws that govern your industry sector.)
- Do you have sufficient knowledge of these areas/laws/regulations?
- Do you know how to implement or comply with these laws?
- What do you need to find out?
- What new documents and practices do you have to develop or revise?
- What sort of legal challenges could you face?
- Do you know what laws apply to this type of situation and how to respond to them?
- Who would you go to for further advice?
- Are there costs involved with complying with regulations? If so what are they?
- Try making a mind map® of ethical and legal matters that concern your business.

10

How to present yourself

The most important thing in communication is to hear what isn't being said.

Peter Drucker, business guru and author, 1909–2005

As soon as we get out of bed, wash, groom, brush our teeth and open the front door, we are presenting ourselves to the world. It doesn't just stop there. When we reach our place of work we respond to e-mails, meet colleagues or clients, possibly attend an interview or make a sales pitch. All these tasks require different presentation and communication skills. As part of running and promoting a business, we are often asked to undertake activities far outside our comfort zone, such as training colleagues who may not wish to be trained, having to give nerve-wracking public presentations and responding to exhausting amounts of e-mail.

This chapter will help you understand not only what you need to focus upon to improve your presentation skills, but more importantly how.

Seven steps to successful presentation

55 per cent of all information we receive we do visually.

Professor Albert Mehrabian, professor of psychology, 1939–

Step 1: Self-presentation

Taking care over personal appearance is the first rule of presentation. It is true that most people make a number of assumptions about other people in a few seconds. Over the years, I found this to be true by conducting regular experiments with mature students. Volunteers were placed in pairs and were each asked to make five assumptions about the other person they did not know, without conferring with them. It was astonishing after just a minute what the students could ascertain about their partner.

The majority of the participants managed to confirm three out of five of their assumptions and a significant minority guessed all five correctly. They were able to accurately state facts about their partner's lifestyle, type of employment, interests and even personal and economic circumstance. **Before the other person had even opened their mouth, they were already sending out messages about themselves**.

This observation will come as no surprise to fans of the Sherlock Holmes memoirs.

> *Pay attention to your hair, because everyone else will.*
>
> Hillary Clinton, senator and US stateswoman, 1947–

A good tip for progress in business is to look the part, by keeping well groomed, looking after your skin, nails and teeth properly. Regularly invest time in shopping for stylish or fashionable clothing. The way you look can unconsciously communicate to others a lot about your attitude and approach to life.

I recall a woman at one of my presentation seminars who had worked for 15 years for the same company. She could not understand why she had not progressed in the firm as other colleagues had. Being promoted to a senior role in a large firm means being on public show and representing the company at international events. This woman, though on a good salary, had a shabby appearance. Her hair was in a terrible state, her teeth nicotine-stained yellow, and she displayed an outmoded dress sense that did not reflect her relatively young age and status.

You don't have to be glamorous or some kind of style guru to be successful (though it does help!). But being a scruff doesn't impress the professional world and won't get you anywhere. Looking stylish doesn't cost much, due to the growth of low-cost tailoring and cut-price fashion high-street stores.

Personal presentation materials for the media

It is useful to prepare for raising your profile in the media by gathering a number of materials that can be used for publicity purposes. A promotional tool kit should include:

- a short profile or biography;
- CV or résumé;
- photographs: pack and product shots, photo of your premises or studio, head and shoulders portraits (colour and greyscale);
- plus photos of you outside your business premises, at your desk or in your studio, with your products, giving a presentation or attending an event;
- informal lifestyle shots of your home with you in them;
- business cards;
- marketing brochure or leaflet, featuring your products or services.

Step 2: Credentials and research

I am to speak for ten minutes; I need a week for preparation; if 15 minutes, three days; if half an hour, two days; if an hour, I am ready now.'

Woodrow Wilson, US President and statesman, 1856–1924

Public presentations

Any form of presentation takes time to prepare. I would advise that if you are requested to present for 10 minutes, it can take far longer to prepare for than if you were speaking for 30 minutes. My rule of thumb is a one-hour talk with fresh content takes at least 10 hours to compose. Surprisingly, I have found that a 10-minute presentation can take just as long, the reason being the amount of thought required in deciding what is important and how to express it succinctly. Public speaking is a vast topic worthy of its own book, but as this chapter exemplifies, any amount of content can be streamlined.

Top tips for presenting:

- Always try to get a good introduction before making a presentation. The intro should outline your achievements and credentials as an authority in the subject.
- Find out as much as you can about the venue and the audience before the engagement.
- When preparing your talk, set out your aims and objectives:
  - Why are you there?
  - What do you hope to achieve?

- Venue: size and acoustics, disability access; what visual and audio-equipment is there and does it work?
- Prepare the room: arrange chairs and tables to suit the purpose: formal, informal, encouraging or limiting debate. Inspect air conditioning, ventilation and access to refreshment.
- Audience: Hostile or willing? Senior or junior staff? Familiar or unfamiliar?
- Expert level or beginners? Single interest or mixed? Older? Younger? Mixed?
- Any access needs for participants with an impairment or disability?
- Discover more about the audience by talking to the organizers, informally chatting to delegates before your turn to speak. Ask direct questions to the audience when taking your place at the podium. If the audience is a large one, conduct quick straw polls by asking people to raise their hands.
- Think of an opening with a short anecdote or story to tell the audience. This will act as an icebreaker, which if pitched appropriately will build empathy and rapport.

First impressions

When attending meetings or giving presentations, either accept the offer of a cold or hot drink or politely refrain. Be decisive.

However, do not under any circumstances eat the biscuits.

Julian Sharpe, senior architect, TP Bennett, 1970–

To cope with important meetings or stressful presentation situations, it is vital to prepare as much as possible by conducting research into the audience or business concerned. **Anyone can become nervous quite suddenly at unexpected moments.** If you rehearse like an actor, your unconscious memory will retain key phrases. This preparation will stand you in good stead if your mind blanks out temporarily due to nerves. It can be a wise precaution to make notes on index cards. Then if recall fails, you can briefly refer to key points and then place them back in a pocket.

When entering a conference hall or meeting room, it is likely you will be offered refreshments. It is important that you avoid dithering and either accept or decline the offer in a friendly manner. This gives an air of confidence from the beginning. It is advisable to have a glass of still water to hand. If cakes or biscuits are provided before or during your presentation, it could be wise to avoid munching on them until afterwards to avoid unexpectedly propelling crumbs at people.

When giving your presentation make eye contact with as many people as you can in the audience or around the table. Try not to focus your gaze too much on one person, as they will become embarrassed and uncomfortable. You may become nervous at times – slowing the pace down a bit will help you to keep your breathing steady and calm.

Step 3: Mindset

Positive thinking can be a major contributory factor to the overall success of your presentation. There are many techniques for developing positive thinking, which we will explore in Chapter 12, 'Keeping positive'. One technique is imagining your presentation as if you were watching a film. The movie is good one, in which you are the star and where nothing goes wrong.

If you have previously had trouble in speaking to large numbers of people, then it is likely your anxiety will increase before the next occasion. If you believe it will go badly, it will. Henry Ford, the American industrialist was famously quoted as saying, 'Whether you believe you can do a thing or not, you are right'. It is all about developing a positive mindset. Therefore, look upon the occasion as a chance to improve. If you have enjoyed earlier experiences in public speaking, then view your next presentation as an opportunity to become more confident.

Dealing with questions

Many students in my public speaking courses over the years expressed real worry about being interrupted with questions which they simply don't have answers to. There are a few useful approaches to dealing with this common situation. Think about likely questions that will be asked about the contents of your presentation. Ask friends and colleagues for feedback on this matter. The last thing you want is to stand in front of a conference full of delegates, with an empty head, not able to answer an obvious question.

To minimize the risk of interruption, one option is to state that due to time constraints there will only be time for questions at the end of the presentation. Another is to acknowledge your own fallibility, with a twinkle in your eye, by introducing your presentation with a caveat – for example: 'This presentation may raise more questions then we have answers to at the present time.'

If a member of the audience asks you a difficult question, try not to let this throw you off course. One way to deal with challenging questions is to try a delaying tactic to buy time. Former British Prime Minister Harold Wilson used to put his pipe in his mouth and light it before replying to a question he was slightly fazed by. Taking up smoking pipes may not be your style, but you can give yourself time to think, by asking the questioner to clarify their question and give more detail, whilst you take a sip of water.

Another major issue is overcoming the fear of public speaking. We will cover this topic further on, but for a crash course in calming nerves see the top-tip list below.

Top tips for overcoming nerves:

- Always eat before presenting. An empty stomach will not help.
- Avoid unusual foods.
- Monitor your breathing. Even the flow in and out and slow it down. Sometimes people find exhaling and then taking in air relieves tension, and inflates their lungs.
- Find ways of relaxing. Some people find doing gentle yoga-like moves can ease tightness in the face, neck, shoulders, ankles and feet. This can lead in to further warm-up exercises to improve posture and voice.
- Drink water with a squeeze or slice of lemon in it; this stimulates the taste buds, and the saliva produced will stop your mouth from going dry. Avoid the usual iced water, as this can shock the vocal cords.
- Write down key points on index cards. You may be able to keep these to glance at while on the podium, or if sitting placed in your pocket.
- If you can't look audience members in the eye, then look at their eyebrows instead. It does work: they don't notice you are not making direct eye contact!

Step 4: Structure

Just keep it simple. In Figure 10.1, I have outlined some simple ideas for structuring presentations. The best structure is to introduce what you are going to say, then say it, and then conclude. If in doubt just stick to three sections.

However, you may have more complex information to present that requires ordering in a logical way. At the beginning of a presentation, either verbally or if using PowerPoint, always show an outline of your presentation; do not have more than seven sections nor more than seven

1. Dream/vision	2. Selling	3. Elevator pitch	4. Proposing an idea	5. Pitching for finance
Let's imagine ourselves a few years down the line (success scenario)...	Interest. Cultivate excitement/ awaken desire about your product or service...	Premise. What is the proposal, idea or venture? Unique features... why special...	Catchy name. Interesting hook line, engage the audience in your presentation, eg samples, opening quotation or question, etc.	What is it? Give a brief outline of business idea, quality of your skills, and relevant experience, associations, etc.
Reality. Now at the moment the situation is...	Risk. Allay or calm any feelings of doubt, eg availability, quality, exclusivity, etc...	Unique selling point. Why is it special? What are the main benefits to the customer or beneficiary?	Make a connection. Stress the key benefits, explain full picture, what is it?	Market. Who will buy this; back up with research/test marketing results.
Journey to dream and steps involved. So how do we get there? Well there are X numbers/things to consider...	Expectations. Convince them it will fulfil their desires, expectations, needs or wants...	Endorsement or testimonials (If you have any). Who approves, supports, stocks or uses your products, etc.	Audience's shoes. Think of the arguments for or against your idea, or the reasons for it: purpose, need, etc.	Strengths/ weaknesses. Tell them how these will be addressed and what the risks are. How will the business make money?
Conclusion. So ultimately our advice is that investing in X is the means to achieving your/our dream/vision.	How to buy. Now? Limited offer? Before stocks run out? Time to collect?	Interested? (Wait for a response before follow-through.) Able to do a deal now, personal appointment, here's my card, your convenience, etc.	Point out the benefits. How things will improve if your ideas are implemented, eg save costs, life enhancing, etc.	Conclusion. Focus on positive messages, and repeat key points only. Then be silent – for questions!

Figure 10.1 Five structures for pitching and making presentations

bullet points on each slide. Most people will have difficulty remembering any more than seven points at a time. This is why, after the area code, phone numbers are no more than seven digits long!

There are lots of ways of structuring presentations. Always draft out an outline, divide it into parts/sections and then points – by topic. The presentation could be structured by grouping activities together under themes, a sequence of steps, relevance, importance, expense, chronologically or other logical ways.

Step 5: Voice

Put somebody you love in the audience in your mind and work for them.

Noel Coward, entertainer and playwright, 1899–1873

Fear of speaking in public is referred to as *glossophobia*, from the Greek meaning 'tongue' and 'fear'. Reading books about speaking in public will not solve this problem. You have to attend presentation skills courses, and seeking advice from a voice coach can be invaluable. Voice coaches usually work with actors, training their voices to enrich and amplify them. Many of those who hold public office and directors of large firms have been schooled in the art of communication.

The main trick with public speaking is to slow the pace of your normal speech down by anywhere from 25 to 50 per cent. The first reason is that in larger spaces, if you speak at normal speed or quicken the flow through being nervous, sound can reverberate around the walls making content inaudible. Second, the audience needs time to absorb what speakers are saying. If content comes out too quickly they will not be able to take it in.

Third, especially when you use a microphone, there can be a millisecond delay to amplification of your voice. This can be difficult to cope with and requires extra rehearsal to master the problem. Speaking too fast can result in filling moments when you are trying to think what to say next, with non-verbal utterances of 'ums' and 'errs'. If you talk too quickly, especially if you are speaking in a second language, your brain cannot keep up with that you are saying. Either take a breath in if you don't know what to say – this will prevent an 'um' – or just pause for a moment. You can be sure that no one observing and listening will notice.

Step 6: Body language

Generally body language takes four forms – awkward stillness or movement, and natural stillness or movement. The awkward behaviour occurs when speakers are either petrified by fear and rooted to the spot, or have so much adrenalin swishing round their bodies that they feel compelled to overly exert themselves. The speakers who behave naturally are those who have overcome their fears, are calm and have a natural style of making subtle or more open, relaxed movements.

When making any presentation make sure you stand with your feet slightly apart, without locking your knees; this will give you more support if you have a sudden attack of nerves. Also, be aware of what your feet and hands are doing. Hold your arms loosely by your sides, with the palms of your hands resting on the tops of your thighs.

When you are nervous, the heart pumps blood into the body's extremities, such as your hands and feet. This can cause hands to shake and make feet perform an involuntary tap dance. It can be a worthwhile exercise to film yourself making a presentation. You can observe any strange gestures in the replay. Become conscious of them, and avoid repeating them in future presentations.

> *I do not object to people looking at their watches when I am speaking. But I strongly object when they start shaking them to make sure they are still going.*
>
> Sir William Norman Birkett, barrister and judge, 1883–1962

Even when you are listening to speakers or attending meetings, avoid slouching and looking bored. It is a small world out there. You could end up working with or being interviewed by the speaker in the future. You wouldn't like to be remembered as being uninterested and apathetic during their presentation. Consider the speaker; it can be very off-putting for them when members of the audience appear uninterested.

One must be aware of other non-verbal communication in the form of cultural difference. The subject is an important and very complex one and requires careful studying. I highly recommend Allan and Barbara Pease's books about body language. It is worth familiarizing yourself with their amazing analysis of human 'tells'. Small hand gestures in one country for instance can mean a very different thing in another. Making eye contact in most countries is a sign of respect. In others it is viewed as disrespectful. Touching and shaking hands is common in most western countries. In others it is customary not to do so. At the time of writing for example, it is regarded as offensive, when greeting Muslim women in traditional dress, for a man to attempt a handshake.

Confidence

Developing confidence takes time. In business life, you will suffer all kinds of problems from bad-hair days to public speaking nightmares. It is essential to undergo such experiences, in order to cope with the problems you will encounter in the future. As Noel Coward commented about acting, it is a matter of 'learn your lines and avoid bumping into the furniture'.

Step 7: Be creative

Merely stating a truth isn't enough. The truth has to be made vivid, interesting, dramatic. You have to use showmanship. The movies do it. Radio does it. And you will have to do it if you want attention.

Dale Carnegie, public speaking guru and author, 1988–1955

Many business people who create PowerPoint presentations find it very difficult to escape from using bullet points and rely too heavily on them. It is fair to comment that having some slides summarizing topics with bullet points is useful. However, having points on every slide is rather uninspiring. Audiences attending such presentations may find it difficult to recall key messages, as monotonous slides blur into a kind of moving wallpaper.

What you need to understand is PowerPoint is a crutch and does not replace the atmosphere that can be created by a good speaker. Think of such memorable orators as Martin Luther King, Margaret Thatcher and more recently Barack Obama. Such great speakers never use PowerPoint. Bullet point presentations are boring and are infrequently remembered.

Some corporate firms do not use PowerPoint as they have discovered they can't interact with clients properly. So instead, they replace the use of technology with a more personal approach, printing their presentation on boards and making use of portfolios. Equally, an explosion in technology has meant there are new options open to those wishing to make their presentations more interesting through the use of animation, illustration, photography, film and sound. **It is worth bearing in mind that hardware and software cannot come up with creative ideas. They are only tools to implement them**.

To make your presentation interesting, to have a strong impact and hold the audience's attention, it's essential to develop creative flair, or collaborate with artists and designers. We will explore being creative further in Chapter 13, 'Creative thinking'.

Table 10.1 gives a number of ideas to help you escape reliance on bullet points.

Table 10.1 Creative ideas for presentations

Photographs	Illustrations	Drawings	Other graphics	Music
Use symbols	Charts	Diagrams	Patterns	Mind maps®
Imagining	Metaphor	Costume	Colour	Change lighting
Props	Drama	Hire actors	Puppets	Magic tricks
Quotations	Humour	Animation	Sound	Demonstration
Audience participation	Refresh the layout of the room	Film/video	Images on boards	Give out free samples
Use an unusual venue	Poetry or stories	Actors and role-play	Dancers	Singing

Improving daily communication

A quick tip list:

- *Phone*

  When making a phone call to a prospective client, after establishing that you are speaking with the correct person, say 'Hello'. Then wait for them to say hello back. Then say who you are and why you are calling. Then wait for them to absorb this information and allow time for them to respond. A mistake many people make in business is speaking far too much and too quickly about themselves; this stifles interaction with the clients from the start.

  When leaving voice-mail messages make them brief, and when leaving telephone numbers, say them slowly and twice. Always be careful about what you say, as you can't be sure who else may be able to listen to that recording!

- *Written communication*

  Always get important letters proofread. If yours is a sole enterprise, re-read letters a number of times before posting them. Always check the weight in respect of franking or number of stamps required to get it there.

- *E-mail*

  It is easy to become overcome by enormous qualities of e-mail. Arrest the flow by not responding to e-mails so frequently in a day. If you slow down, then everything else will.

Try to limit e-mails to a maximum of 50 words – if you are sending complex instructions, pick up the telephone and make a brief call instead of wasting time writing long replies.

Avoid e-mail fights. I bet everyone regrets sending at least one e-mail in temper. Either don't respond at all – that is, don't fuel it – or if it becomes a problem and you wish to resolve it, phone the sender to see what the 'misunderstanding' or 'confusion' could be, or reply by post.

If you are struggling with e-mails, let people know you are inundated and agree an e-mail acknowledgement code, by just simply pressing the reply button and typing 'Thank you', 'No problem', 'Sorry can't do', 'Phone me' or 'Noted'.

● *Web*
Remember when posting articles or comments onto the internet that they may be there for years. So be careful what you decide to fling into cyberspace.

Closing thoughts

Finally. Present on Tuesday.

Paul Arden, art director and author, 1940–2008

This famous quote by Paul Arden sums up his theory concerning the best time to pitch ideas. This is touched upon again in Chapter 11, 'Negotiating a better deal'. In short, Arden discovered that by the end of the week clients had forgotten Monday, and by the end of Friday they hadn't had time to absorb the later presentations.

Key points

● Take care in your personal appearance.
● Research and prepare carefully for any presentation situation.
● Fight the fear. Learn to control nervousness through warm-up exercises.
● Keep presentations and the message simple.
● Take a few risks with your presentations to make them more interesting.
● Don't continue to kid yourself about those bullet point presentations.

Enterprise skills booster

- Next time you have an interview or are going to make a presentation, go to the hairdressers and treat yourself, whether a man or woman, to some pampering and grooming. It doesn't matter how soon or far away the date is, go and book the appointment now. Make a note on your wall planner.

- Start creating your promotional tool kit of marketing materials and photographs.

- Make sure everything is in hard copy and can be stored digitally on pen-drives or CD ROMs.

- Enrol on a presentation skills or public speaking course.

- If you can't afford that, stick a mirror to a wall and practice introducing yourself or rehearse a presentation.

- If you have a video camera, put it on a stand and film yourself standing up making a two- to three-minute presentation. It could be about anything, how to cook a pasta dish, recounting a holiday or describing your best friend. Pick any topic you can easily talk about, where you won't need to refer to notes. The point of the exercise is for you to observe your body language, tone of voice, speed of delivery and so on.

- Pick a number of objects from around your home or office, a paperclip, child's toy, Post-it notes, etc. Now have a go at composing a 30-second sales pitch, and then practice selling them to friends or colleagues.

- Think about how you would like to be introduced to an audience. What three key credentials would you like to have mentioned: your job or business title, previous companies worked for or founded, experience, achievements, awards, prizes? Draft out a few lines you can give or send to organizers of events, so they will know what to say when you give your presentation.

11

Negotiation

Why does Professor Geremek never get wet when it rains? Because he negotiates between the droplets.

Anecdote about Bronislaw Geremek, Polish statesman, 1932–2008

Negotiation, like business law, is a huge topic and difficult to do justice to in a relatively short chapter. However, the themes discussed in this chapter provide an overview of mastering the art of negotiation. This skill is vital in order to prosper in business, especially in a competitive marketplace. Adopting an entrepreneurial mindset to making money is essential.

Bartering is an ancient skill, and was the only method of exchanging goods before the introduction of minted currency. With the invention of money, it has become all too easy to equate products and services in terms of monetary value alone. People generally make the common mistake of narrowly focusing on trying to get the highest price, rather than see what can be gained from taking in the full picture.

It requires a great deal of practice to gain proficiency in subtle methods of persuasion. You may have experienced small victories, whether from haggling over produce in a marketplace or solving conflicts between feuding siblings. Negotiation comes into play every day, from planning an evening out with friends, through to sharing responsibilities at work. It is about achieving mutually beneficial outcomes, through discussion and bargaining.

In business as in life, you don't get what you deserve, you get what you negotiate.

Dr Chester L Karrass, founder of Karrass and author, 1923–

This famous quote from Chester Karrass, the negotiation supremo, is a simple realistic observation of human attitudes to reward. You have to value your skills, and have the confidence to argue a case. In the rough and tumble of business life you have to know when to say no. Self-confidence is an important factor to ensure success in negotiations.

Win–win, win–lose, lose–lose

A camel is a horse designed by a committee.

Sir Alec Issigonis, engineer and designer of the Mini, 1906–1988

To broker a deal it is essential that both sides are content with the agreement reached. Pleasing everyone can be a tall order. Usually most people will concur that when the majority of the conditions are met on both sides, the result is win–win. The 'win scenario' for all parties generates genuine goodwill. This is an invisible asset in building partnerships and relationships.

However, when we unveil our product, no one wants to see a camel when the intention was to construct a horse. Business owners or managers of average ability may view success as gaining all their goals at the expense of others. Entrepreneurs and businesses managers often enter into unhappy agreements, perhaps because they are under financial pressure and have few other options available to them. It is important to remember that win–lose situations are no foundation for happy long-term working relationships. You can be storing up problems for yourself later on.

A lose–lose scenario is not usually a good outcome for either party. Deals that fall through are as important as the more successful ones, because they are valuable learning experiences and help develop negotiating skills. It is worth considering why opportunities were lost. Perhaps too many demands were being made upon the other party. If the approach to the situation had been slightly different, could a deal have been agreed? Conversely, perhaps the demands made on your business were simply unrealistic, and it was a wise decision not to enter into the agreement.

I recall a negotiation session with a firm that went sour. The firm was making far too many demands on my business for the remuneration involved; I left the table with no contract. At the time, I felt upset that we could not reach an acceptable agreement. Then 12 months later, I read that the firm concerned had gone into insolvency. None of the consultants who worked on the project were ever paid. Had I agreed to the contract offered to me, my business would have become insolvent. Making poor decisions in contract negotiation can have disastrous consequences, which includes bankruptcy.

Preparation

The most difficult thing in any negotiation, almost, is making sure that you strip it of the emotion and deal with the facts.

Howard Baker, senator and statesman, 1925–

Mindset

Before you begin any negotiation, whether face to face, by phone, or via e-mail, you must think through the entire proposition in detail from beginning to end. A mind map® will help you understand all the factors involved, by making associations through words, doodles and diagrams. This exercise will enable you to formulate ideas, questions and anticipate problems.

To help you think through the process, the mind map® at the end of the chapter includes all the key themes addressed. There may be many more specific to your situation. This will necessitate the use of larger pieces of paper, to make space for other aspects. Try not to be daunted by the number of factors to be thought through. It requires a large amount of practice to improve cognitive abilities in processing and remembering all the issues concerned. **The mind map® will anchor the key issues and arguments in your own mind**. Drafting them out will help you to make a logical, well-presented or strongly argued case. Completing mind maps® on earlier topics such as understanding 'the mind of the client' and 'how to sell' are essential prerequisites to prepare for the further stages outlined in this chapter.

When completing a mind map® always summarize key points on a note pad. This can be useful to refer to in meetings, especially when discussing complex projects. It can be just as useful to keep notes by the phone in case the client should call you. In the commercial world, initial confirmations of interest and acceptance may be made in only a five-minute phone call. The caller will expect that you will be organized, that the proposal has been analysed, and that you are willing and able to do the work within budgets and deadlines. This is why being able to check current and future work commitments on wall planners and having a pre-prepared list of queries will speed progress along in concluding a deal.

When we are offered small opportunities we might be able to make up our minds quickly. But as business ventures become larger, whether in terms of scale or risk to the company, it is crucial to devote more time thinking through strategies carefully with senior managers and team members, before undertaking any commitment.

Negotiation theory and practice

> We may not be able to get certainty, but we can get probability, and half a loaf is better than no bread.

C S Lewis, novelist, 1898–1963

The theories outlined here are based upon Bill Gates' 'principles and tactics' of negotiation, summarized in Steve Mariotti's *The Young Entrepreneur's Guide to Starting and Running a Business* (2000). We will then go on to explore how these are applied in the 'Seven steps to successful negotiation'.

Principles

Goals

Research and thinking time are vital to preparing your mindset. Your goals need to be clear. **What do you wish to achieve from this negotiation?** Make use of cards or blank postcards to clarify your thoughts. You may find it helpful to make key headings on different coloured cards. This can help in remembering key points.

Mind of the client

Think about the situation from the other person's point of view. If you were them what would you wish to achieve in their position?

It is likely that you would wish to achieve the best deal. For a buyer, usually the goal is to pay the least amount of money, for the largest amount of work completed, or goods delivered in the shortest time.

What do you think their minimum and maximum requirements will be?

If selling products or charging fees for services, your goal will be to gain the best price, usually for the minimum amount of effort, and undertake the work or fulfil the order in a comfortable time frame.

Consider what is important to them and what is not important to you. Think about what may be not important to them but could be very important to you.

Example of what's unimportant to you…

If a customer is haggling about the price of an order, one of the main extra costs on top of the order is the delivery of goods to their premises. They are being difficult and don't want to pay for transportation, nor go to the hassle of picking it up themselves.

You may have a van, and happen to be travelling near to the delivery point the next day. However, they don't know this, do they? You could in this particular instance reluctantly offer to deliver the order yourself, next day free of charge, if they agree to pay the original price for the order.

Negotiation is a different set of skills to building rapport. If this were a different circumstance, you would be happy to deliver goods and nurture good relations. It is important to realize when it is right to negotiate terms. If you continually offer to do extra chores for customers or clients for nothing, then it is worth considering that you may be taken advantage of. Hard-hearted business people simply exploit kindness as a weakness.

Example of what's important to you…

To illustrate the alternative situation of something being unimportant to the client but important to you, let us look at the provision of a recommendation in the form of a product endorsement or testimonial. Many new businesses need client testimonials or to be associated with other reputable businesses. It can be highly advantageous to have your business connected with the names of celebrities, established entrepreneurs or other key players in your field. So for example, having permission from organizations or firms to make links from your website to theirs can help build trust with new clients or suppliers.

Securing public endorsement from satisfied customers is promotional gold dust. Gaining quotes from named sources is vital to any fledgling business. It only costs the satisfied client or customer a few moments of their time, yet this can make a big difference to your business prospects. When you ask their permission to make web links, or provide testimonials, try not to give the impression that you are desperate for them. Just ask in a friendly manner if they would be willing to provide a quote. If you feel uncomfortable about asking new clients for a recommendation, simply include their name in a client list on your website and marketing materials.

Disclosure

It is crucial you avoid disclosing to the other party what is important or unimportant.

Even if something seems insignificant to you, it still can be offered up in return, to win concessions from the other party. Early on, the other party has to think that they have won some points, when in reality the conceded matter was of no concern to you. This is valuable when in turn you wish them to give ground later on. It is about both sides showing willingness to compromise to come to a mutually acceptable agreement.

Showing enthusiasm in business is usually advantageous. However, it is worth considering occasions when revealing excitement will lose you the upper hand. For example, if you are overly keen to sell, a buyer may sense desperation and put in a lower offer.

Best and worst

The final principle is to figure out what your bottom line is. **What would be the best/ worst outcome for you?** What are your own minimums and maximums? What would be the highest fee, with the most resources and length of time required? What would be the lowest price, with least resources and shortest amount of time you would agree to?

It is crucial to go in at a high price or within market rates when quoting professional fees for any business opportunity. As explained in Bill Gates' 'tactics', failure to understand this principle may result in your undertaking work at a less than adequate profit margin or even making a loss. However, as you will see in the scenario below, between a novice and a master, if there is enough flexibility on the point of agreeing a fee, other opportunities can be brokered. Though a tough bargain was stuck, the veteran was wise enough not to 'push the envelope'.

Novice and the master

I recommended a client to a web designer who had recently started her business. I failed to mention to the designer that the prospective customer taught negotiation skills for a living. Later I considered the designer should be made aware of this, as the lecturer might use her skills to barter the fee down. By the time the designer received my warning, it was too late. The designer responded with news that the client had already forced her down to her 'lowest fee', and was unhappy. The negotiation lecturer detected this and realized she was nearing a win–lose scenario. Knowing this would not be beneficial in the long run, the lecturer offered in return for good work to recommend her services to several businesses that required a web designer.

The designer learnt from this experience, and in the future would resolutely avoid overly compromising her rates. She finished the commission to a high standard. The client was thrilled with the result. Fortunately, for the novice, the client was true to her word, and this slightly dispiriting experience resulted in a significant number of new orders at full commercial rates.

Simple scenario

A good analogy for negotiation is the selling of a second-hand car. It is unlikely a buyer would expect to pay the first price quoted. The vendor will have factored this likelihood in to the advertised price, knowing they would be willing to reduce the price by anywhere from 10 to even 25 per cent, depending upon how anxious or eager they were to make a sale. The customer might be willing to pay the asking price, if they think the car is worth it. Equally, the seller may be persuaded to make further discounts, if offered 'hard cash'!

Tactics

I don't think you can negotiate, unless you can think yourself into the position of those you are negotiating with. Think to yourself, how are they thinking and why are they doing what they are doing?

Sir John Major, British Prime Minister, 1943–

Obtaining all the facts

Frequently, agreeing a price is not as simple as selling a second-hand car. In business dealings, clients frustratingly may be not forthcoming about what they are willing to pay. This is because they are trying to close the best deal, by forcing you to reveal your position. So if initially they don't wish to state what they are willing to pay or receive straight away, then go with a reasonably extreme quote – eg very high if selling, very low if buying – and sound pretty confident about it.

Therefore, one of the main purposes of negotiation is to make or save as much money as possible.

When selling products or services, be prepared for clients who will try to barter fees down. It is in the salesperson's interest to defend profit margins.

When buying, it is a duty to get the best price available, to maximize yours!

Silence

Use silence as a tool; the other party will then be sure to say 'Yes', or 'No' or 'Yes, but…' Then listen to their objections or argument. As part of your menu of stock phrases, add, 'and the budget is?' Always try to get this in pretty early on, and if they do reveal a figure, even an invented one, then you can quickly assess the viability of your participation. If an unrealistic amount is being offered, and there appears to be no other advantage for becoming involved in the deal, then opting for a lose–lose scenario may be sensible, to avoid wasting any further time.

Bargaining and compromise

If the project offers other long-term advantages, this is where thinking through the situation comes into play. How can effective compromises be reached? This is where one considers all the 'seven steps' involved in the negotiation process including the different 'minimums' and 'maximums'. (Refer to page 136)

● How can you initiate a bargaining process?

● What can you give up or offer to improve the deal?

Recall the earlier story about delivering goods yourself to avoid losing an order and possibly a customer. The barrier to successfully completing the deal was only a small disagreement about transportation costs. Is there something you would not mind giving up that would make the opportunity worthwhile to your business?

Whatever the client suggests, you must think of other counter offers that could be put forward to improve the deal, or sacrifice elements to gain ground on other more important parts of the proposal. It is important that you gain the most from negotiation, such as the best fee, the most time and resources. As we will explore later, money may not be the most important consideration. It could be gaining credit through association or public exposure, or having extra time to complete the project instead.

Stock phrases

Always be prepared with a number of 'stock phrases' to use, if a new client should unexpectedly make contact about a possible commission or project. You always need to buy as much time as necessary to consider any proposal before making a decision. If clients should approach you by telephone, always ask them to confirm details by letter or e-mail (it may not be necessary of course). This tactic will generate a small delay to allow for further consideration. If it is a simple proposition and e-mail isn't required, just say that you are 'about to go out', or are 'finishing off some urgent work' and agree to 'call them back' either within the hour, or later in the day.

Write a few of these 'stock phrases' down. They must be convincing and not off-putting. For instance, never say to prospective clients 'Sorry, I am too busy'. I have even seen some start-up businesses stating this on their websites! Never tell anyone that you are overly tied up with work, as people will start saying to each other, 'Oh don't contact them, they have enough on', and before you know it incoming enquiries will cease.

Establish the means of sharing work with others in the event of being fully committed, or ascertain if the commission is non-urgent. Customers may be willing to wait a bit longer for their order. Avoid turning down any work. If the opportunity offered is simply not of interest to you, try to be helpful by recommending another contractor.

Dealing with difficult players

Don't worry about using silence as a tool. It can give each party time to think about offers made, or cause them to reveal more about their position. If negotiation grinds to more than an uncomfortable pause, be prepared to fill it by thanking them for considering you; that you would like a little time to think further about this interesting proposal, etc. When would a convenient time be to get back to them, either later that day, or the next? If they respond with, 'We would like to know now because there are other suppliers interested', this is a pressure tactic. Either accept the offer or turn it down. Beware; if this is how the client is treating you at the beginning of the relationship, their attitude is not likely to improve. If it is not a good proposition, politely thank them for their interest and let them know it is not right for you.

If they don't try to force a decision, it's likely they want you for the job, and will readily give you time to consider the proposal. Perhaps, if they appreciate your reservations, they might be willing to improve their offer. Therefore, it is quite possible they will also find a few extra hours useful to consult with others, and get back to you with an improved offer.

Presentation

It is difficult to negotiate where neither will trust.

Samuel Johnson, writer and lexicographer, 1709–1784

Before we discuss the seven steps to successful negotiation, as well as preparing your mindset you need to think about presentation. As mentioned in Chapter 10, 'How to present yourself', from a personal perspective make sure that you are well groomed and wear appropriate clothing. The formal attire of business does not necessary fit all situations. In fact wearing clothing at odds with the situation can serve to alienate. Suppose, for instance you are breaking bad news to employees about the firm not being able to give them any pay rise this year. The announcement will not go well if you appear in front of disheartened workers looking recently tanned, dressed in casual sporting wear or an expensive designer suit.

Attitude

One must enter any form of presentation or business meeting with a positive mental attitude. If you come in exuding confidence, demonstrated with an initial handshake, attentive body language and enthusiastic manner, then you are already halfway to clinching the deal. First impressions are very important, as discussed in the previous chapter.

Using humour can ease tensions, though if applied clumsily it can create them. If you are a naturally witty person, then a few light-hearted moments during the course of discussions can lift the mood and spirits of those present. However, knowing when to make the odd quip is a balancing act. If you're unsure, it is wise to keep any jokes for later celebrations.

As we have mentioned earlier, becoming emotionally agitated about business concerns makes it less easy to present your case in a coherent and rational manner. However passionately you feel about an idea or issue, emotion can deflect your argument and weaken your cause. When one party becomes upset or even angry, it can force others to concede. However, it is more likely that people will reconsider their own position, and call off further discussion.

Avoid sowing seeds of doubt

If there are any weaknesses with your proposal, such as manufacturing faults, legal objections or other issues, it is best to acknowledge such problems or obvious flaws in the early stage of your presentation or opening remarks. Don't leave out such matters or mention them only at the end. Concealing them will only store up trouble for later on. Avoid addressing risks in concluding comments, when people tend to be more attentive. There is a danger only the bad points will be remembered rather than a previously well-argued case.

Environment

Location is another vital part of feeling comfortable when liaising with other managers or business owners. The further away from your usual surroundings the more uncomfortable it can be. Try to arrange any face-to-face meetings at your own premises when possible. It is far easier to nest in your own domain and circumvent the hassle of travel. Internet conferencing is an easy solution, though not a substitute for meeting in person.

However, there is something to be said for seeing prospective clients on their own ground in order to gauge their organization's size and style. When you are starting a business, your offices or the back bedroom may be embarrassingly unimpressive. It is possible to impress visiting clients by hiring venues. It is worth examining the approach of the Saatchi brothers, when starting their advertising agency in the early 1970s. They realized the most important part of gaining high-profile clients was to give the impression they were already successful. They achieved this by employing an element of theatre. When they knew a client was visiting, they famously dragged people off the street and paid them to sit in their rented offices for a few hours. The freshly press-ganged recruits were requested by the brothers to look busy whenever clients arrived.

If kidnapping people from the street does not appeal to you, then perhaps it is better to arrange an alternative venue. This is where hiring rooms at membership clubs or at professional bodies can be helpful. If neither of these is an option, then meet at the client's premises, and be as relaxed as you can in unfamiliar settings.

Seven steps to successful negotiation

My father said, 'You must never try to make all the money that's in a deal. Let the other fellow make some money too, because if you have a reputation for always making all the money, you won't have many deals.'

J Paul Getty, industrialist and oil magnate, 1892–1976

Step 1. Time

Recent research by psychologist Debbie Moskowitz (*Guardian*, 2007) establishes that there is a rhythm of behaviour through the working week. From her studies, she has established that workers are more open to negotiation on Thursdays. However, on Fridays, most likely due to waning energy levels, they are more likely to make snap decisions! Therefore, it is worth once again thinking about the mind of the client and opt for mid-week business discussions.

Time can be your most valuable asset. Always try to gain as much as possible to complete orders or meet deadlines. One has to factor in extra time to allow for mistakes, wastage and absenteeism from illness, either your own or that of team members. Having more time to complete work may allow your business to undertake other projects at the same time, as flexibility has been built into the programme of delivery.

However, this may not always be possible; the client could be under pressure to meet a deadline. If this is the case, then you may have to sacrifice weekends, or have to pay for extra assistance to complete the project within the desired time frame. This arguably could increase costs and be reflected in the final quote. For example, dry cleaners and printing firms usually charge nearly double their usual prices on express services.

However, outside the traditions of such high street traders, when dealing with customers, taking advantage of the situation by overly inflating your fee unless justified, could damage goodwill built up over the years and result in the loss of future orders. You could be unwittingly forcing a win–lose situation, as the client has no time left to find another supplier. It is better to say something along the lines of 'I would usually charge £X amount, but because you are such a good or new customer, I will only charge you £Y instead'. Other options include offering 'just over' standard rates on rush jobs.

Step 2. Resources

If the deal is not as generous as anticipated, then see what the client can offer in the form of resources. This could take many forms and may fall within their 'unimportant' category, but be 'important' to you.

Depending on the context, and the scope of the client's activities, they may be able to provide a variety of products and services that may enhance your side of the bargain substantially. Clients may be able to provide free materials, research facilities, temporary storage, transport, travel, accommodation, workspace, hosting of events, or access to equipment, software and marketing services though their database, mailouts, and company reports.

A good example of exploiting resources is a business student who wished to set up a furniture business. One of his main problems was paying for transport of goods around Britain. He realized during his research that home removal firms frequently moved people's worldly goods to and from different towns (usually, for the vast majority of journeys made, the lorries were empty either when going out or returning). In negotiation with various removal firms, he brokered a deal whereby some of his deliveries were made by empty lorries. They stopped off to pick up goods from his workshop, and then dropped them off en route. A small sum of money was paid to cover petrol costs, thus reducing overheads for his own and other businesses.

End note

If you are offering an ungenerous fee then enter into the spirit of barter and be aware how valuable your own resources could be to the other parties.

Step 3. Money

When presenting fees and quotes to clients, it is wise to offer a range of products or services in different price bands. Suppose for instance that you really would like £5,000 for this order, but you suspect the customer may not be willing to pay that much. Therefore, in your initial quote or during negotiation, it can be advantageous to offer a proposal at £10,000, with another at £5,000. This principle is known in the social sciences as 'perceptual contrast'.

Psychologists Zakary Tormala and Richard Petty (Goldstein, Martin and Cialdini, 2007) undertook a great deal of research into the subject of persuasion. They discovered that when a customer is presented with an expensive complicated offer, and a simpler, less costly one (say for £5,000), the client perceives the £5,000 to be far more reasonable when compared with a more costly option. This may make them more willing to pay £5,000 when presented with a high-cost alternative.

To avoid issuing or receiving ultimatums, either offer or ask for quotes on a sliding scale. So for instance, the fee is between £5,000 and £10,000, depending on what is required.

Always be aware in any selling context that the customer may put in a lower offer than the fee or price quoted. You should always prepare for this situation. Try not to react by saying 'no' to customers who ask you for a discount. Saying 'no' just closes down the possibility of a sale and the opportunity to persuade the customer to value the product or service. It could be the case that you would be willing to give them a slight discount if they purchased more products or services than originally requested. A customer, for instance, may offer to buy a £50 product for £40 (which you won't entertain), but you could persuade them to buy two products retailing at £50 each for £90.

Step 4. Rights

It is so easy to be fixated with the money issue as a 'flat fee'. One needs almost to rediscover medieval cunning when discussing the subject of licensing brands (trademarks), products (design right/patent) or artwork (copyright). **If you don't understand what intellectual property is, then it's impossible to negotiate licensing rights**. The Association of Illustrators in the UK and The Graphic Artists Guild in the United States both publish books that explain legalities, royalties and fees. These guides are essential reading for visual creatives, managers and business owners who wish to license trademarks, or commission designers, photographers, artists, designers.

It is vital to understand how long-term incomes can be generated through merchandising, manufacture and reproduction. They are achieved by negotiating a percentage of sales in the form of royalty payments. Having a flat fee for all your rights today is not comparable to accruing the same fee, through licensing rights, every six months for the next five years.

It is important that inventors, product designers, business owners and artists, where possible, do not sell or assign their intellectual property, in the form of patents, design right, trademarks and copyright, but rather exploit them through licensing. A licence is a contract that grants others the right to reproduce images, designs, songs and the like, and is made up of three factors: time, use and location. An example would be the right to reproduce images for three years, on children's T-shirts, in the UK only.

As mentioned in Chapter 9, 'Legal and ethical matters', laws including intellectual and industrial property rights vary around the world. **You must know and understand the rules governing this area before undertaking any initial negotiations with manufacturers, investors and buyers. Being naïve will get you nowhere in business.**

Step 5. Risk

Those with a Machiavellian approach to business will try to shift risk on to the other parties. It is up to conferring parties to spot this type of activity during negotiations, and find mechanisms to deflect liability. For many reasons, particular aspects may not be sufficiently covered during this stage, so check all clauses in any contract offered. Before signing, one has to be certain that the written agreement reflects the spirit of the verbal one.

A common anxiety is unevenly weighted payments, as for example when contractors promise large penultimate payments following a long programme of delivery. This could cause enormous cash flow problems for your business. To avoid this liability, opt for payment in instalments at key stages during the project.

Another example is heavily weighted fees offered on difficult parts of contract delivery, with the result that you have to achieve exceptionally high targets. The likelihood of achieving these could be too risky. If the other party will not give ground on this issue, you may decide not to commit to the project, as the terms are too demanding. It is worth stating you might be willing to agree, if there is a 'get out' clause, giving you the option to pull out later on.

Penalties and liabilities take many forms and sometimes they are not obvious. Many entrepreneurs for instance can be caught out when venturing into renting business premises. It can be a shock to discover, usually due to insufficient scrutiny of the lease, that as tenants they are liable to pay both rent and repair costs on the property to the landlord for the full term of the lease, whether they occupy it or not. This could mean liability for many tens of thousands of pounds spread over several months or even years. Good news for the landlord though!

Step 6. Power

The power to have the final say is frequently obtained by restricting that of others. This can pose a terrible dilemma for freethinking entrepreneurs. As soon as your business starts to grow and takes on other directors or partners, your own powers concerning decision making will diminish.

When you seek large amounts of investment, from business angels or venture capitalists, they not only buy a share of your business but the right of veto. As soon as the principal shareholder owns less than 51 per cent of a company, they no longer have control. The 1 per cent in 51 per cent is worth a lot more in real terms, than one hundredth of the share value.

Whatever the circumstance, if you fear loss of control, it is worth arguing the case to retain as many rights as possible in implementing your own decisions – though trying to persuade business investors with the dominant share to relinquish power may be pretty fruitless.

However, if new business partners enable your business to rapidly expand and increase turnover, then having to cope with short-term restrictions will be worthwhile from a financial point of view.   .

Step 7. Goodwill and credit

It is wise to give acknowledgment and retain goodwill in business relationships. When this is lost through shabby treatment or through lack of acknowledgement, then the long-term future of working relationships can be jeopardized. Resentment in one party may begin to fester.

For example, if a manager has made a short-term gain by screwing another business down to its bottom line, then it is likely the supplier will not be predisposed to invest further effort in the deal. There may be a problem one day, for instance, and the manager urgently needs assistance, perhaps needing extra products for an important order, or unexpectedly requiring work done to meet a deadline. He calls the supplier last minute on a Friday afternoon, expecting them to pick up the phone. The jaded party decides not to. They listen to his panicked demands, and unconcerned, they ignore the call.

Alternatively, in another inappropriate move, a manager decides to take all the credit for the success of a project, thus ignoring the talents of other hardworking parties. The consequence will be that the other businesses may decide not to work with the manager on future assignments.

Always build rapport with your collaborators, and always make sure they are fully credited for their contribution. It is pure folly to do otherwise.

Can't reach agreement

The first thing to decide before you walk into any negotiation is what to do if the other fellow says no.

Ernest Bevan, politician and statesman, 1881–1951

Forcing a decision or lose–lose

There is nothing worse than negotiating with arrogant or tiresome people who are unwilling to bargain. The point is reached at which you realize that you are not going to close the deal. To resolve the situation by introducing a 'third party' is a risky strategy but a possible one. Calling on a 'third party' makes it plain that there are other interested buyers or suppliers. The likelihood is that this move will either overcome the stalemate by forcing an admission, or end the relationship.

Bluff

In 1973, Universal Pictures refused to release an early George Lucas film, *American Graffiti*. To force a decision, Francis Ford Coppola, who produced the movie, jumped up at a studio screening of the film waving a chequebook in his hand offering to buy the movie on the spot. Fortunately for him, his bravado worked, and the executives released the film (Kao, 1989).

Closing thoughts

The go-between wears out a thousand sandals.

Japanese proverb

For managers, it is important that teams who have been successful in clinching contracts should be rewarded. Celebrating is a good way to mark achievement and enthuse staff. Equally, if the team failed to make a deal, then commiserations are in order – best not to remind the disconsolate of Zig Ziglar's famous observations on losing, 'that nobody wants to come to a pity party!'

Key points

- Undertake as much preparation as possible before entering any form of negotiation. Write key points on cards or in a notebook.
- Always aim for a win–win scenario.
- Know your bottom line.
- Don't just focus on the money; try and think through the wider issues and implications of any deal.
- Always be conscious of your presentation, be confident and value your products and services.
- Do not be cajoled into instant acceptance or refusal. Always read the contract, and clarify mysterious clauses.

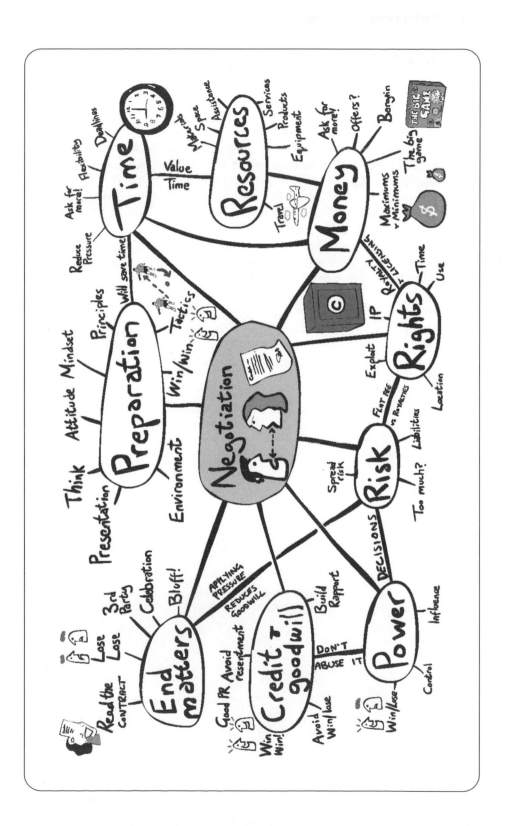

Enterprise skills booster

Negotiation can only be learnt by practising. Included here are a few tips to help you get started:

● Try swapping personal possessions, products or time in the form of services, with friends or other traders.

● Join a local 'time bank' or other 'barter' schemes. Just type these phrases into a search engine to find local or countrywide projects. If you don't find a time bank initiative in your area, you know what you have to do don't you!

● Whatever situation you are in think about the topics outlined in this chapter, including the seven steps. For example if you are an artist, musician, writer or designer, brainstorm with some friends about how many ways your images, words or sounds can be used (Table 11.1 may give a start).

Table 11.1 Example of how a musician could commercially exploit songs (add your own suggestions)

Download i-pod	CD	Film soundtrack	Advertising
Ringtone	Cover versions	Radio – live sets	Lyrics reproduced on T-shirts
Jingle	Band/image merchandizing	Remix	Performance rights

12

Keeping positive

We are all in the gutter, but some of us are looking at the stars.

Oscar Wilde, playwright, 1854–1900

In the course of business life, there will be many problems to face, including fighting the odd battle. When experiencing difficulties, it is best to cultivate an optimistic outlook. Retaining a sense of humour can help you and your team cope during periods of uncertainty. Positivity is related to perception: the neurological process of observing and interpreting our surroundings. Some may for instance perceive the conditions of the gutter as horrendous. Whereas others will be relieved they are not residing in the sewer!

Mindset

Nothing can stop the man with the right mental attitude from achieving his goal; nothing on earth can help the man with the wrong mental attitude.

Thomas Jefferson, US President and statesman, 1743–1826

There is much published work on the subject of positive thinking, a portion of which can be best described as psychobabble. Many books and individuals make unrealistic claims that their 'techniques' will guarantee future success, claims that are not substantiated by independent research.

Developing a positive attitude is much more about applying common sense in your general approach to life. It is unrealistic to suppose that people can solve problems or obtain goals by indulging in activities such as repeating, mantra-like, 'I will succeed' 1,000 times. This can be an essential focus exercise for athletes to boost personal morale and raise adrenalin levels, but achieving progress within a business context demands a completely different approach. It is not sufficient to simply 'believe' you will be successful. There has to be real analysis of what you wish to achieve and why.

As you may have realized in reading this book, practical application of action or business plans requires the acquisition of a great number of qualities and skills. Ambition and enthusiasm can power you along the route to success, but without being fully aware about a wide range of matters your energies can be misdirected.

Environment

The trouble with this job is it is like having a thousand people kicking your back-side morning, noon and night.

Tony Blair, British Prime Minister and statesman, 1953–

Surroundings and experiences will shape people's character and outlook on life. Hardship for instance can toughen individuals or equally break them. Social mobility is another important factor. It can be very difficult to excel in life if you don't have good guidance, education, financial support and opportunity. There are many examples of people rising from humble backgrounds against the odds to become public figures and successful business people. Present-day self-made people include entrepreneur and politician David Davis, businessman Duncan Bannatyne, entertainer and entrepreneur Dolly Parton, all now multi-millionaires but who grew up in poverty. If you really wish to succeed in life, you have to be willing to go out and create opportunities for yourself.

In 1990 the British Prime Minister, John Major, aspired that Britain should be a 'classless society', just as historian James Truslow Adams in the early 1930s spoke of 'The American Dream': an aspiration that any American 'could become a millionaire'.

All success is relative to circumstance. What an individual thinks or feels as success is unique to him.

Alfred Adler, psychoanalyst and author, 1870–1937

It is important to the process of developing a positive outlook that you do not compare yourself too much with those who achieve an extremely high level of recognition in their field. Of course, it is valuable to find out how they achieved their ambitions, which can be useful to further your own strategy. But it is highly likely you may discover that they had more advantages and better opportunities than yourself. We don't all get the same life choices! If for instance you grow up in a remote small town, it is unlikely you will be exposed to the same influences as those living in big cities or in other parts of the world. It may be the case that you simply do not get the right chance to manifest your talents.

All things are relative to circumstance so don't be discontented with your own achievements. If you have tried your best, then that is all you can do! Value and enjoy the progress you have made so far.

Other important factors to consider are facing prejudice on grounds of gender, class, appearance, race or religion. These issues may not affect you in any way, but if they do, then it can be a great obstacle to overcome. It is better to be fully aware about discrimination in whatever form. Failing to gain an opportunity may have nothing to do with your ideas, talents or skills. Try not to become disheartened and let such rejection destroy your confidence or faith.

> *Never give up on your dreams, as you never know what is round the corner. At least if you can say you gave it at least 100 per cent, it is better then living with regret.*
>
> Dame Kelly Holmes, athlete and Olympic champion, 1970–

The solution may be simply a matter of persistence, that suffering prejudice fires your spirit to fight on. Equally, endless rejection can become very dispiriting, so view options rationally, change direction and do something else.

A good example of how it can be impossible to succeed in your chosen field is that of male ballet dancers who train from childhood, but fail to grow tall enough for any production to consider them for a leading role. Young girls face a similar challenge when the opposite occurs and they grow too tall. The dancer has to face the reality of the situation sooner rather than later, and find a new direction.

There may be other opportunities within or outside the performing arts, such as joining experimental dance companies, acting, choreography, teaching, or perhaps becoming a model or retraining to be a fitness instructor. The length of a professional dancer's career can be over by their mid-thirties anyway, so, if you are a dancer, it is wise to keep your options open whatever height you are!

Life balance

We all have varying expectations of daily life. There is much evidence that a balance of work, rest and leisure activities aids positive thinking. Further time should be devoted to friends and family, and maintaining good health by eating nutritious foods and keeping fit. Having a good life–work balance can certainly increase well-being. Likewise, I have observed many business people who are truly contented and happiest when running their enterprises. As in many lifestyle businesses, it can become difficult to separate work from leisure activities, as all aspects of living can contribute to the business in some way.

It is important to develop an approach to work that you find enjoyable. If you are fully content with filling in VAT returns on Christmas Day then that's fine. However, if this has arisen from taking on too many personal responsibilities, then act now to ensure that future Christmases are paperwork free.

Self-belief

> *If you don't believe in what you are doing 100 per cent, you won't succeed.*
>
> Alan Sugar, entrepreneur, 1947–

It is important to nurture a spirited attitude towards your objectives. Self-determination and belief are qualities that need to be combined with other skills to ensure success. To make progress you must spark the fire of ambition in your belly, and become an 'SIF', a 'single issue fanatic', be totally driven and focused.

> *When you are screwing up and nobody is saying anything to you anymore. That means they have given up. This is a really bad place to be.*
>
> Professor Randy Pausch, professor of computer science, 1960–2008

However, it is essential in the pursuit of a vision not to become blind to constructive advice or criticism. Over-confidence can develop into arrogance. Quick success can easily encourage cockiness! Be careful, during your quest, at whatever stage, not to ignore the views of others that initially you may not recognize as helpful.

Dealing with rejection

Because the greatness comes not when things go always good for you, but the greatness comes when you are really tested, when you take some knocks, some disappointments, when sadness comes, because only if you have been in the deepest valley can you ever know how magnificent it is to be on the highest mountain.

Richard Nixon, US President and statesman, 1913–1994

When embarking on new ventures, it is possible you won't get them right first time. **Try not to regard things going wrong as failure. View them as testing an idea that didn't work out on this occasion.** Think of the great inventor Thomas Edison and his 10,000 failed experiments. Be resilient to rejection, and simply see it as part of the process.

It is important to establish why particular business ventures don't work out. There could be a number of factors, including fending off fierce competition. Consider the acting profession. There are thousands of actors applying for very few roles. The famous actor Oliver Reed displayed his own enterprising solution to such problems. He discovered that going to parties and chatting up secretaries who worked for casting agents was a perfect shortcut to ensuring his CV and photograph appeared at the top of the pile for film parts.

It could simply be the case that too many other businesses are targeting the same market as you. Equally, your business idea or product may be so innovative that investors or customers are simply not ready for it. James Dyson (2002) for instance, who now has his own factory and research facilities in England, spent years trying to interest UK manufacturers in his Dual Cyclone innovation. Eventually he gained support abroad for licensed production of the first dyson® vacuum cleaners.

Alternatively, as with the mischievous Oliver Reed, there may be a more creative approach to securing openings that you just haven't thought of yet.

Cultivating a positive mindset

Keep away from people who try to belittle your ambitions. Small people always do that, but the really great make you feel that you, too, can become great.

Mark Twain, humorist and writer, 1835–1910

Activities to avoid

- Keep away from overly pessimistic or aggressive people. Long-term exposure to such people can leave you with a negative outlook.
- Try not to associate with people who take recreational drugs, and don't take them yourself. Taking drugs has a very unpleasant effect on people's health, personality and perception of the world.
- You may not have much of a choice, but avoid if you can depressing environments such as dirty, dusty and cluttered home or workspaces.

Activities to do

- Find people who are engaged in similar activities to yours and share your enthusiasm. Being with humorous, optimistic, clever people can be a good long-term positive influence.
- Try to maintain a healthy diet; eating too much fatty and high-sugar food can cause problems with concentration and decrease energy levels.
- Make the most of your work and home environment. Try everything from following a regular cleaning rota, and buying a few potted plants, to undertaking a complete refurbishment and revamp. If you are going to spend a lot of time in a particular environment, it is a good idea to make it as comfortable as possible.

Closing thoughts

Do the thing and you will have the power.

Ralph Waldo Emerson, poet and philosopher, 1803–1882

It is vital that you seize the day, whether you have a large schedule of work or nothing in the diary. If you don't have any orders, for instance, get on the phone and call people up, send out promotional packs and generate some opportunities. Even if you spend all day or a whole week working on advertising your business, if it generates one lead or sale that is one more than you had before.

If you are feeling in low spirits about your business, go and talk to your friends or professional advisers about what can be done to turn the situation around. Sometimes taking a break can help you get things into perspective. Go for a walk, or if simply worn out, take the week off. You will come back revitalized and in a much better frame of mind to solve any business problems.

There is an old adage in business: when the phone keeps ringing it is easy to believe it will never stop. But when it does stops ringing, it is quite possible to convince yourself it will never ring again. Don't let any down period put you off track; fill the time usefully by undertaking research, applying for opportunities or undertaking fresh initiatives, designing marketing materials and getting those accounts done!

Key points

- Examine how other people in your field have built or run their businesses. Is there anything they did in the early years that you could try?

- Have a realistic look at all the obstacles you may have to overcome, and work out if there is any way round the problems you may face. What, if anything, can be done?

- Consider what magic event you would like to happen that will take your business to the next level. Could it be getting some kind of break? Perhaps meeting new contacts? Gaining an award?

- Start making a plan of how you would set about working towards accomplishing this.

- Have a think about how your living and workspaces can be improved. If having a quiet week for instance, invest in a few cans of matt emulsion and a roller or two and spruce the place up a bit.

- If your business has been failing for some time, or you can't get your business going, why not try something different?

Enterprise skills booster

There are numerous tools to help develop a positive mindset or outlook. You will find below a number of exercises. Please note these are only suggestions and readers may find particular exercises more useful to do than others.

● *The 'Magic circle of confidence'*

Some people find this a useful exercise to boost self-confidence. It is based upon an NLP (neuro-linguistic programming), 'Circle of excellence' exercise.

Imagine you are going to make a presentation, go into an interview or talk to a customer. When you have to assert yourself or handle a difficult situation, whatever the reason is, try the following to get into a positive mindset:

Imagine there is a magic circle in front of you....

Close your eyes and recall, sense and feel the following...

Step into the circle and remember the last time you felt truly happy...

Figure 12.1 The 'magic circle of confidence'

Step out

Step into the circle again and recall the last time you felt truly relaxed...

Step out

Step into the circle yet again and recall the last time you felt really confident...

Step out

Step into the circle once more and recall the time when you were very focused...

Step out

Now step into the circle for the last time and join all these feelings together...

'I am happy – relaxed – confident – totally focused'

Hold the feeling, remember how this feels and open your eyes...

● Make a timeline of all your achievements in the last few years. You will see there have been other times in the past where there has been a gap between major successes.

● Think about all the good decisions you have made in the past, write them on Post-it notes or make a list. Look at it every time you feel a bit fed up.

- At the beginning of every week, look back over the previous one and think about what went well and what didn't.

Is there anything you could do next week to build on successes?
For ventures that did not go so well, is there anything different you could do next time to achieve a better outcome?

- Visualization can be a useful tool. Before undertaking any venture, negotiation or presentation, try to image the situation as a short film. Thinking through the process, picturing how you or your products appear, what you will say when, and so on.

- When was the last time you celebrated your success?

If you haven't, why not treat yourself, and perhaps friends and family to a day out, or go for dinner at your favourite restaurant?

13

Creative thinking

Some painters transform the sun into a yellow spot, others transform a yellow spot into the sun.

Pablo Picasso, artist, 1881–1973

There are many theories that have been put forward by philosophers, psychologists and scientists attempting to define or describe what creativity is. In relation to enterprise, I am sure most readers would agree that creativity is using the imagination, or other approaches such as play, experimentation or brainstorming to come up with original ideas.

Creativity, simply put, is about how we use knowledge to achieve new or unexpected outcomes.

Christopher Frayling, Rector, Royal College of Art, 1946–

Creativity originates from the Latin 'creare', meaning 'produce'. A large proportion of people only associate creativity with the 'arts'. Likewise, many business people narrowly define it in terms of the ability to 'solve problems'. There is another perspective on this interpretation. It is usual for corporate leaders to refer to 'creativity' as 'innovation'.

Why is it needed?

Creativity is to conceive new things and having the zeal to implement them.

Professor John J Kao, enterprise guru and author, 1950–

Whatever your view, it is vital from a business point of view that creativity results in a viable product. This could be achieved by putting good suggestions into practice, or making that biro sketch a working proto-type. Many companies invest in creativity and call it *Research and Development* (R&D), though it doesn't always lead to a viable product. (It is worth being aware that substantial investment in R&D is tax deductible. Equally, micro-businesses and sole enterprises can claim tax relief on research, such as business trips, visiting fairs and events, etc.)

Being able to think in a creative way is vital not only to survive but to thrive in business. When you are running a business, you have continually to think of new ideas and solve problems. If you are a manager, then I am sure you will agree that you don't just have to sort out your own prob-lems, but face a stream of daily questions from your team members, seeking guidance or opinion.

How is it cultivated?

Creativity involves breaking out of established patterns in order to look at things in a different way.

Edward de Bono, creative thinking guru, 1933–

Environment

To encourage creativity, it is important to give some thought to your envi-ronment, and think how design could make your office, factory, retail outlet or studio an inspirational place to work. Design is an essential element in improving the quality of the workplace atmosphere.

At a basic level, your business needs to have well-lit spaces where people can regularly meet to discuss ideas, and equally, where individuals can contemplate alone. If you don't have access to such facilities, perhaps on sunny days make use of the local park. If this is not feasible, there will surely be suitable spaces in local business, community or arts centres, libraries, or even cafés that you can use for a short time.

There are a number of conditions that when applied together can foster a more creative outlook. Theorists such as Carl Rogers (1954) point out that the best conditions to stimulate creativity should 'lack rigidity', and people should be 'able to play spontaneously with ideas, colours, shapes and relationships'.

What hinders creativity?

Time constraints are another important issue that has been examined by the psychologist Richard Wiseman (2004a and b, Chapter 3) in his experiments exploring creativity and how people spot opportunities. He has proved that if you put people under pressure to be creative then output dramatically decreases.

This was demonstrated by an experiment where he asked two separate groups to create as many doodles as they could in tiny boxes. One group were told they had three minutes and another were informed they just had one minute. The participants started on the exercise. However, both groups were requested to stop after only one minute. The group which had been told they had three minutes had produced twice as many doodles as the group that had only been given one minute. They both in reality had the same amount of time, yet the group that believed they had more time, actually was the more productive.

How creativity is stimulated

Therefore, to stimulate creativity there needs to be the provision of a suitable space with interesting activities for yourself or your team to do. These could be in the form of brainstorming, challenges, playful exercises or experimentation. Also, be sure to give participants plenty of time to enjoy the experience.

The mathematician Henri Poincaré, in his famous creativity theory, suggested that 'eureka' moments often happen after there has been an intense period of study or thought, and that the brain takes time to think about a problem before original ideas can be formed. So don't be overly disappointed if a brainstorming session isn't as fruitful as you hoped. It may be sometime later when soaking in the bath, sunbathing on the beach, or sitting under a tree when that good idea will come to you!

Making creativity pay

Making creativity cost-effective is a difficult operation to undertake. It is about striking the right balance between pace of production and meeting deadlines. In all explorations, investing time and money is a risk. It might well be the case that the prototype is not viable. Equally, it could be that progress in development is so slow that competitors beat you to the marketplace. It is worth considering that on some occasions this is no bad thing. Coming to market in second place may in fact help you to make sales, as your competitor has undertaken a great deal of hard work in cultivating demand; thus making it easier for you to launch a similar service or product.

Ideas

An invasion of armies can be resisted, but not an invasion of ideas.

Victor Hugo, novelist, 1802–1885

Developing a lively mind and being able to come up with interesting ideas is a specialized skill. An ability to come up with clever suggestions will always be valuable. If you are launching an entrepreneurial venture, then being unoriginal or copying other people's ideas will not get you very far. Your approach has to be unique so that your business will stand out from the crowd.

Good examples of innovative companies are Innocent, Ideo, Google™, 3M™ and Virgin. If we just touch upon one of these companies: the design firm Ideo are selling their 'Method Cards', which can be purchased from their website. The cards each describe a creative exercise to help designers explore new concepts. The fact that they are freely selling this tool is quite a groundbreaking move in itself. Selling the cards is a high-risk strategy as they are giving away their own product development knowledge, not only to the world but to their competitors.

These companies and many similar to them really value creativity as a vital component of sustaining their businesses. They channel resources into developing imaginative products and services and striding ahead of the competition. Their customers recognize and value this. They appreciate new and exciting products. **Originality is achieved by taking a few risks, by investing money into research and employing inventive people**.

Visual artists, designers and inventors have developed the skill of being able to think 'out of the box', that is, to find ingenious solutions. Many creative professionals think in conceptual ways: they are able to formulate good ideas. In any enterprise, large or small, these attributes are vital. Being an entrepreneur requires developing your own creative mindset and working with other talented people. Anyone can learn to be more creative, but it is sensible to recognize the high level of expertise that graduates from the top art and design colleges and universities have amassed. These individuals have the aptitude to come up with many innovative ideas and solutions.

Being resourceful

Necessity is the mother of invention.

Plato, philosopher, 428–347 BC

During the Second World War, due to food shortages, Britain's civic parks and private gardens were turned over to growing vegetables. Women devised meals made up of leftover food. In response to clothing rationing, they tinted their legs with boot polish, and drew a line up the back of their legs to imitate the seams of stockings.

Creativity is often at its best when there is a limitation of money, materials or resources. This encourages people to improvise, invent and use their imagination. However, it is not a good excuse to underfund initiatives. People can be resourceful for a certain time, but if they are subjected to long periods of struggle, frustration will set in and undermine future progress.

When starting a business you need to draw on as much support and resources as possible, at home and in your local area. Most people have home computers and personal mobile phones, which can be relied upon in the beginning for basic admin purposes. It may be that you have only a small amount of money, so that hiring, borrowing or buying second-hand equipment is the best option. Bartering and sharing costs with other business, exchanging skills or products to get websites designed, buildings decorated and workspace subsidized can be invaluable.

Local universities, innovation hubs and business support centres are also useful. I recall when studying part-time at a university that my student card gave me free access to expensive equipment, software, a photography studio, a library, technical support and helpful lecturers. Over the years I have met many mature students who were running their business either at a college in incubation units or on an ad hoc basis, by being able to use equipment in the workshops worth tens of thousands of pounds, which start-up businesses could not get access to anywhere else. Don't ignore these organizations when setting up in business. You may be very surprised to find out what they offer.

Creative problem solving

Problems cannot be solved by thinking within the same framework in which the problems were created.

Albert Einstein, theoretical physicist, 1879–1955

There are a wide range of business problems that have to be solved on a daily basis. Ongoing issues include gaining and keeping customers, coping with intense competition, time pressures, stretching budgets, pitching for work or finance and making successful presentations. (A plethora of business problems are featured in Chapter 2, 'Understanding risk' in Table 2.1, in the form of risk analysis.)

What sort of creative solutions are there to typical problems?

As you can see from this book, mind mapping and doodling can help you understand situations and identify the issues that you need to think about to gain a successful outcome. Using words, doodles and pictures will help you remember information easily.

People can lack confidence in drawing as they think they can't do it. It is worth thinking about what the purpose of the sketch is. As I explain to students in my creativity workshops, it doesn't matter how rough or badly drawn things are. A commercial artist, photographer or designer will be able to turn any simple pencil drawing into a professional image or diagram. The point is to get the idea drafted on a piece of paper and then develop it from there.

Different creative solutions

Here are three different problems that show how creative thinking can result in imaginative solutions. The first story is about utilizing resources, the second is about brainstorming and using creative thinking to solve a problem, and the third suggests how visualization and making analogies can make presentations more memorable.

Starting a business with little money

A middle-aged man who had been unemployed for a long period of time needed advice about how to set up his business. He had many technical skills and a nice personality, but was at a loss as to how he would get his business started.

In discussion, I helped him realize the resources he had and to maximize their use. The man had a house, a car, a wife and two teenage sons. Over a few months, the events described below took place.

He needed a van to start his business, and after a discussion, he found a friend who was willing to swap an old transit van for his car. He also needed storage space for stock. The friend now had more space in his garage and allowed him to use it to store goods for the next six months.

Most of the family home was turned over to running the business, even making use of the kitchen table!

The man's elder son had recently completed a course in web design. So his father commissioned him to design the company website. His wife worked part time in a bakery. He managed to persuade her of the merits of undertaking a bookkeeping course at the local college. She then under-took the weekly role of doing the accounts. The man's younger son found a new source of pocket money from helping his dad to wrap, pack and post items to customers.

Apart from the costs of insurance and some other expenses, the man managed to set up his business for very little outlay with the resources that surrounded him.

Making equal opportunity forms less divisive

There was a young woman who was very unhappy with the standard equal opportunities form that her organization was using, whose box system she found divisive. The visual impact of a grid does not convey any sense of commonality. I am sure many readers of this book have experi-enced these types of forms, and you may have felt the same way about them. (For those that are not familiar with 'equal opportunity forms', they are a classification system to monitor inclusivity upon grounds of gender, nationality and ethnicity.)

After a period of creative thinking, exploring what shapes expressed inclu-sivity and well-being, we decided on the circle. We removed the bound-aries of the boxes and placed the ethnic categories within the friendly symbol of a circle. Figures 13.1 and 13.2 demonstrate the concept.

Coming up with ideas in a more imaginative presentation

A lady who worked in the sugar cane industry wanted to make her pres-entation more interesting. Her PowerPoint slides showed production rates

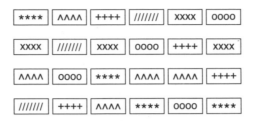

Figure 13.1 Standard equal opportunities arrangement

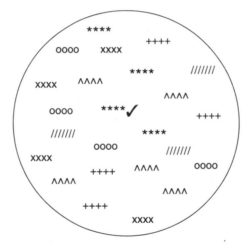

Figure 13.2 New idea for a more unified arrangement

and sales in the form of dreary plain bar charts. After a period of creative thinking, she realized the resemblance between the shape of the sugar cane and the bars in the chart.

Making use of analogy, symbols and metaphors when explaining facts and figures is more entertaining than plain charts, and helps the audience remember. In most contexts connecting visual images with a subject will make more of an impact.

The initial idea was to replace boring bars with illustrations of sugar canes. This idea has all kinds of possibilities, such as animated presentations depicting growing cane that represents increasing sales. Other ideas worth exploring could be using lumps or spoonfuls of sugar as symbols of volume or amounts. Alternatively, she could display replica models of cane cut to different lengths to get messages across in a far more exciting way.

Note to managers and trainers

If you are making regular presentations, sticking to a regular formula can be a sensible strategy. However, it is important to realize that if visual materials are not regularly refreshed, your message will become stale and uninteresting.

Publicity stunts

> *Inspiration can come from anywhere.*
>
> Richard Branson, founder and CEO Virgin, 1950–

The most entertaining and cost-effective approach to promoting any business or capturing the attention of an audience is through devising imaginative publicity events or unusual methods of communicating a message. Publicity stunts are in effect mini-performances, to which the media are invited by a press release or photo call.

Stunts can be anything from a few students standing in fields dressed up in pantomime horse and cow outfits, to bizarre global advertising campaigns. In presentation situations, being creative can pay off. An entrepreneur called Levi Roots appeared on the UK investment television series *The Dragons Den*. He captured the hearts of the panellists by singing a song about his financial needs. It resulted in him being offered £50,000 that kick-started his business. Jamie Kennedy, an American actor, discovered the only route to gaining parts in films was to become his own agent. He invented a character called 'Marty Power'. His impersonation of this fictional agent opened many doors into the film industry that he couldn't under his real identity.

Getting your business in the news

When starting out, or even running an established company like Virgin, stunts are press-friendly ways of gaining TV or newspaper coverage of a business or product launch. Publicity stunts can be a relatively inexpensive means of reaching a wide audience.

Richard Branson has commented in books how publicity stunts built the Virgin brand, and they still are one of the company's main methods of promotion. He has featured in an extraordinary number of stunts over the last 40 years. He has even risked his life, when a high-altitude hot air balloon stunt went perilously wrong. Virgin later capitalized upon this near-death experience by starting a new enterprise offering balloon flights!

It is a good idea to fake your publicity stunt before it happens, to capture some good quality photographs – the reason being that if you are a small business, it may be unlikely the press will turn out to your event, even though invited. Press releases, with stunning photographs attached, are much more likely to capture media attention, if the images are eye-catching and of professional quality. Journalists may well publish them with a few descriptive lines scooped from the release. It is a good policy to contact reporters by phone before posting or e-mailing anything. Feature desks can become snowed under with press packs. The *Guardian* newspaper in the UK for instance receives hundreds of press releases every week. They may only pick one per day to feature, and it's most likely to be one with an interesting photo attached.

A good source for ideas and learning more about creating memorable stunts can be found on the website of the public relations firm, Borkowski PR. Interestingly, Mark Borkowski (2000) has created attractive picture books on the subject, exploring the history of creative advertising to the present day.

Closing thoughts

Grasp the challenge of management with both hands and really make it a creative expression of who you are and what you believe.

Mike Southon and Chris West, authors of *The Beermat Entrepreneur* and
other books, 1953–/1954–

If you believe you are not a naturally creative person, then learning to use your imagination and come up with new ideas can be hard. To be an entrepreneur it is vital to develop foresight and visualize the future. Otherwise, there is a danger your business products or services will become stale and outmoded. The pace of consumer trends and technological change is accelerating. Young people leave schools and colleges every year. Many of them will wish to start a business, making use of their new skills and energies. Therefore, it is vital to learn to be innovative and always be planning your next move.

Key points

- Creativity is the life breath of enterprise. Examine aspects of your business. Brainstorm problem areas and write ideas down on Post-it notes, put them on a board or wall. Keep a little notebook or sketchbook to hand for jotting down ideas when you are out and about.

● Analyse what barriers there are to developing business and personal creativity. What can be done to change the situation?

● How could you become more creative? What new activities could you do in your free time to stimulate the imagination? Visiting a museum? Art gallery? Theatre? Taking up cooking or art classes, joining a choir or forming a band? Going on a trip to the seaside, countryside or to your capital city?

● Is it possible to make changes to your workspace or regular routine? If doing the same activities at set times every day with the same people, then it is unlikely that new approaches or ideas will be cultivated.

● What kind of creative people or specialists would be able to help you find creative solutions to your business problems? Illustrator? Designer? Architect? Artist? Inventor? Photographer? Musician? Actor? Creative consultant? Marketer?

● Consider how you could make use of publicity stunts to promote your business. What type of media coverage would be useful? Local or national newspapers? Lifestyle magazines? Industry periodicals? Radio or television coverage?

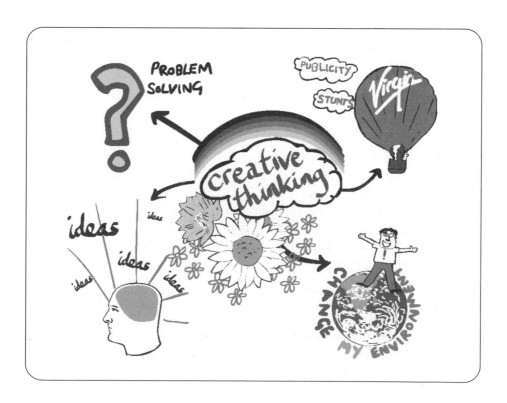

Enterprise skills booster

There are many creative thinking exercises. Here is a selection that you may find interesting to try. Some of them are more fun when working in teams.

Brainstorming

This is usually a team activity, but it can be done alone. There are many types of brainstorming approaches. Typical formats include placing an object such as a brick on a table and asking the group to think of (and state) all its different uses. Usually there is a time limit, perhaps 3–10 minutes. Ideas should be free flowing from contributors, and not be analysed or dismissed as silly. The suggestions are written down quickly by a facilitator on a large piece of paper. Later on, selected ideas can be chosen to debate further. If a group is new to brainstorming, then using a 'brick' exercise is useful as a warm up.

Brainstorming can be used to explore more important issues such as projects, action planning, marketing ideas and product development. It is an essential tool in encouraging the process of creative thinking.

Inventing a new product

This exercise helps in developing creative skills, including brainstorming, drawing and presentation skills.

Spend a few minutes thinking about each of the following:

- Think of a...
    - material, eg soil, sand, fabric, steel, brick, wood, paper, plaster, plastic, etc;
    - shape, eg circle, square, triangle, rhomboid, octagon, blob, etc;
    - form, eg cube, sphere, pyramid, structure, moulded, modelled, slab, etc;
    - functioning object, eg lamp, bicycle, umbrella, bed, chair, etc.
- Now pick one word from each section, eg 'wood', 'circle', 'moulded' and 'lamp'.
- The challenge is in 15 minutes to design, and present on an A1 piece of paper, a 'lamp', using 'wood', a 'circle' with a 'moulded' form! After 15 minutes, the teams present their products.

Analogy and metaphor exercise

Another useful exercise to nurture visualization skills, to understand problems and make connections is to do the following:

- If your business or product...
  - were a colour, what would it be? eg Blue, gold, magenta or green?
  - were a food, what would it be? eg A lemon, coffee, chips or curry?
  - were a place, what would it be? eg Desert, modern city, river or in outer space?
  - were a vehicle, what would it be? eg Taxi, classic car, van, glider or rocket?
- Place your four words together. Is there any word you would like to change and why?
- For instance, your business is currently like a clapped-out car, and you would like it to become a hot air balloon. How would this change affect your company's business plan, USP, mission statement, ethos, branding and presentation?

The £10 challenge

This is a great exercise to try, for individuals or teams. To make it interesting, teams could come up with ideas in a brainstorming session. Other options include giving a further period of time to put the idea into practice – a day, week or month. Each person or group would make a small presentation about the outcome, the next day or later in the month.

If I gave you £10 or US $20, how could generate publicity for your business?

(It is worth noting you don't have to spend the money!)

The puppet show

This is an imaginative exercise that encourages resourcefulness, creativity, presentation and time management skills. It is also a lot of fun!

In 25 minutes, a small team has to write and produce a three- to four-minute puppet show, making puppets and props with anything to hand, such as paper cups, pens, drawing faces on fingertips or shadow play. In 25 minutes the team has to agree a storyline, make puppets and rehearse. After which, the teams should be ready to perform their show!

Planning your next move

Entrepreneurship, in my definition, is a spirit – a quality – that believes so strongly in an idea that it risks the security of the present for the reward of the future.

Gorden Engdahl, retired Vice President, HR, 3M™ Company, 1920–

Running any form of enterprise is a risk. To achieve outstanding accomplishments in life requires the courage to defy convention to a greater or lesser degree. Entrepreneurs, artists, scientists and inventors who create innovative products or make groundbreaking discoveries have been prepared to make sacrifices. They have taken risks, with time, money and resources, to search for the fruits of success. But if temperament and determination are necessary, they are not enough. Planning for the future is essential if your business is to grow. **Without an action plan, there is no focus**. It will become impossible to measure progress or prepare for growth.

The innovator

A small bakery found it could not compete with the number of local supermarkets baking their own bread. The bakery owner realized that the business would have to close if he didn't do something drastic. He undertook some market research and identified a growing demand for novelty cakes, so he wrote a business plan and applied for a £150,000 loan from the bank. He re-equipped his premises and spent months re-training staff. His novelty cake firm is now one of the major UK supermarket suppliers.

If the owner had not taken a risk and invested in a change of direction at that particular moment, the bakery would have shut down. Instead it became a vibrant, successful business.

Goals and vision

It takes 20 years to make an overnight success.

Eddie Cantor, American entertainer, 1892–1964

It may take much longer than you anticipate to fulfil a major goal. The more industry knowledge and enterprise skills you acquire, the more likely it is you'll succeed. To ensure this, find the right people and environment to work in. If you are running a sole enterprise you must find like-minded people you can call on occasionally for assistance. In time, you may decide to join forces to form a team-enterprise. It is important to embrace innovation. Don't close your eyes to the advancement of competitors, nor the pace of technological change. If you wish to run a business in the 21st century then you have to face such challenges.

Researching future opportunities

The future will not just happen if one wishes hard enough.

Peter Drucker, business guru and author, 1909–2005

The business you start or currently manage may not be recognizable in a few years' time. As experience grows in running an enterprise, you will realize there are aspects that are enjoyable and others which are not. You may find that some difficult tasks can be taken on by others – freeing up more of your own time to focus on what interests you. As the months and years pass by, you will find that certain ventures work and others don't. It is likely as you continue to plan your personal and business future, that changes of direction will be necessary.

Try not to view any early failed initiatives as mistakes – venturing into the world outside the security of university or employment can come as a shock. If you look for guidance, no one person will have all the answers, and several advisors will be necessary to help you on your way.

In this milieu, you have to cultivate future opportunities. At exceptionally busy periods during the year, this can be difficult to do. Depending on your business model, opportunities could be self-generated by approaching companies or clients/customers directly, or applying for contracts or tenders.

As mentioned in the last chapter, finding time for research and experimentation is vital. Google™, for instance, encourages its engineers to devote 20 per cent of their time to creative projects. This is what eventually led to their online astronomy initiative, Google Sky™, and previously Google Earth™. The Japanese believe that managers should not spend more than 25 per cent of their time on operational matters. If managers fail to find time to solve problems and think creatively, then the Japanese would regard it as poor time management (Boulden, 2002).

Therefore, as mentioned earlier, don't just rely on traditional approaches for business generation. Try creating your own initiatives.

Importance of innovation and technology

In the future, there will be no web designers, as everyone will be able to do it themselves.

Rodrigo Zuniga-Andrighetti, entrepreneur, 1978–

The quotation above is from one of my students, who by the end of a short business course had managed to win an award and set up a company. I believe this to be a highly astute observation of the rapid pace of technology-based businesses.

Nearly 20 years ago, web designers could earn a fortune, as they were in short supply. Today the job pages in any broadsheet newspaper require basic website updating skills, or more advanced levels of design. With new web design software packages, 'build your own' deals and online social networking sites, even a beginner can create a web presence in a few minutes. There will always be a need for specialist web design, but whether present day web design companies will be able to sustain high profit levels in the future is another matter.

Whatever type of business you wish to start or manage, it is essential to understand how innovation can assist or damage the future prospects of the enterprise.

First, innovation can be a big problem: failure to observe developments in your field may result in you throwing in the towel, or in the worst case going bankrupt. Hi-tech machines have easily imitated traditional skills for many years, quickly and cheaply. Britain has unfortunately lost the majority of its manufacturing base. This is a big problem for UK entrepreneurs, inventors and product designers. They can prototype their ideas at innovation centres, but then have trouble getting them into production. Innovators have to resort to manufacturing in other countries to ensure costs are kept low and retain realistic profit margins on the wholesale or retail prices.

Reusable paper is already possible; it uses e-ink contained in the paper by micro-encapsulation technique. The next step would be to print wires and transistors on paper to form circuits, so that a radio receiver could be integrated with the paper. This device could be run on solar energy.

Professor Susan Greenfield, visionary author and neuroscientist, 1950–

Second, it is important to understand how rewarding your own explorations into investing time and resources in innovation could be. It doesn't have to be technological to be innovative. It could be a matter of developing new ways of making or doing things. Consulting with engineers and designers about the latest methods of presentation, production, processes, materials or construction can be helpful. There may be all sorts of reasons why you should innovate; below are a few suggestions.

Why invest time, money and resources in innovation?

- Keep ahead of the competition.
- Bring new products or services to market.
- Find new approaches to management and formulate decisions.
- Solve problems.
- Improve productivity, save time, costs, manpower or energy consumption.
- Create original marketing and promotion campaigns.
- Attract investors, partners or new clients.
- Change direction.

Whatever your reasons for exploring new ideas, you have to be prepared for a degree of uncertainty about outcomes and be willing to put in a great deal of hard work. Innovative businesses have become so because they take on higher levels of risk then others that simply service market demand.

Managing growth

Plans are only good intentions unless they immediately degenerate into hard work.

Peter Drucker, business guru, 1909–2005

Growth is achieved by the combination of business planning and market demand. If there are many competitors in the market, to increase market share you will have to think how you can win over your competitor's customers. If the market is stagnant or shrinking, then it may be wise to innovate and change direction.

The fledgling sole enterprise

When you are starting out it is still possible to develop a team of expertise. This can be done through informal networks or buying in assistance. As a sole or micro-enterprise, it is more likely that help will be bought in, for instance, a business adviser, accountant, solicitor and perhaps even marketer. It's quite possible you will have creative suppliers, such as graphic or web designers, illustrators or photographers, who contribute to the branding and promotion of the business. Even when you are working alone as a sole enterprise, there may be at least 10 people you can contact for assistance. It's impossible to start a business in isolation. Other experts are like a 'talking' mind map$^{®}$. It can be the case that these suppliers will help you consider ideas from different perspectives. Make good use of them. A simple consultation will mean better-informed decisions.

Team enterprises

For a small business the flexibility of buying in expertise such as services on a regular basis can be fundamental. However, budgets cannot stretch to experts being employed on a full-time basis when they are only required occasionally for ad-hoc contracts. This is where the course of expanding resources through taking consultants on as 'associates' is advisable.

Associates are engaged by contract. Don't worry if immediate sources of work are not available to offer them. They are usually freelancers or other sole-director companies who work for a number of businesses. Seasoned associates are aware that work offers vary.

The cons...

Make sure your associates are bound by appropriate contractual terms relating to confidentiality and competition. Be aware that associates also run their own businesses, and will sometimes work for your competitors.

The pros...

The added benefit of contracting others in this way is there is a team available that can be called upon at crucial times. Many businesses that consist of one or two people can give the impression, by their promotional materials, that a large specialist team is available. This can be a route to business growth and minimizing costs at the same time. Once again, make use of your associates. They will be happy to give their views if it improves the likelihood of future work opportunities.

The larger enterprise

As a business grows, owners may decide that taking on the competition is not an appropriate move. As discussed earlier, embarking on discounting prices to encourage sales is not a wise strategy. Price wars, for example, whether by a number of bars in town centre offering endless 'happy hours', or airlines flying people to Tenerife for the price of a biscuit, are simply not in anybody's interest.

The result of price wars between bars is an influx of binge drinkers for short time periods, though with no real profits being made. Publicans face increased costs of cleaning and repairs from disturbances fuelled by cheap alcohol, which, to add insult to injury, may well scare away any regular patrons. Harsh price wars between airlines result in companies being pushed out of the market, which in turn means less choice for passengers.

Collaboration

Businesses may decide not to compete for all their sakes, deciding instead to identify strategic alliances partnerships or in some cases even merge with competitors. For instance, there are two reprographic firms near my home. Both have photocopying machines. One shop concentrates more on high-volume photocopying orders. Whereas the other, down the road, offers customers the use of a photocopying machine for occasional copies. However, its main business is printing posters and other promotional materials. The two shops have an informal agreement to direct appropriate clients between the two businesses. Without this cooperation, both would struggle, as there is simply not the demand for two identical services being on offer in such close proximity.

Businesses are sometimes better off working in tandem, so that together they can thrive side by side in a competitive marketplace. Please note that informal agreements between small traders are not the same as 'price fixing' or 'anti-competitive behaviour'. There are plenty of reprographic outlets in the area, and they all charge different prices for their services. These two shops are simply agreeing to refer potential customers requiring different, though to some extent similar services, and by agreeing a few ground rules they can both continue to trade independently, but potentially more profitably.

Future opportunities

The best way to predict the future is to invent it.

Alan Kay, architect of the Graphical User Interface, 1940–

Unfortunately, there are no time machines (at present!) to see what the world will be like in 10 years' time. **Whatever the future holds for your business, be prepared to change direction**. You may currently be surrounded by opportunities but fail to recognize them, as they are not what you envisaged, and so you disregard them. This can be pure folly. To make sense of business it's essential to develop an enterprising, flexible and commercial outlook. There are no rulebooks for entrepreneurs or intrapreneurial managers, only potential and future possibilities.

Key points

- If you haven't an action or business plan for the next 12 to 36 months then set about creating one. (For a larger business, a 5–10 year business plan is advisable.)

- After reading this book you may have come up with some new ideas about future aims and objectives. If so, revise your plan accordingly.

- Buy some books about the subject of innovation, make contact with your regional innovation hub, and attend talks about developments in your industry sector.

- Examine your business services and products. If you had more money how would you invest it and why? This may help you define what areas require updating and refreshing.

- Most sole enterprises wait until work overload happens, before realizing they need extra help. Contact a business adviser or consult with your accountant about how to take on an assistant. Alternatively consider other start-ups that are still building their customer base. There are many newly self-employed people who would value a few days' work a month to help support their own businesses.

- If yours is a larger enterprise, is it worth merging with other companies to cut overheads and increase market share?

In conclusion

I hope that you find this book an entertaining way of learning new approaches to business and practical enterprise skills. If you are feeling a bit overloaded by the weight of information, try to focus on a few chapters at a time. The 'Enterprise skills booster' exercises have been tried and tested over 10 years. The best way to practise new skills is to apply them, so please give them a go! If you have any suggestions or feedback, please feel free to send me an e-mail at info@makingsenseofbusiness.com. Your thoughts will be most welcome.

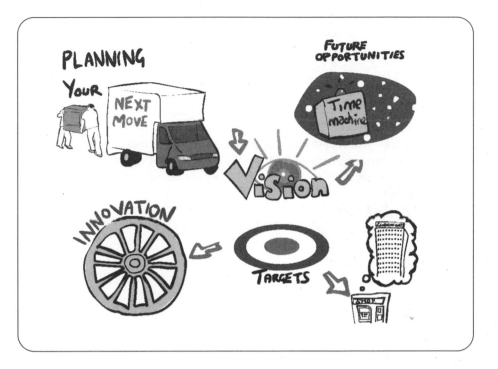

Enterprise skills booster

Many of the exercises in the last chapter also function as innovation exercises; here are some more.

- What will...
    - be the headlines in the newspaper next year;
    - consumers want to buy in four years' time;
    - social/cultural/lifestyle or technology needs be in five years' time;
    - be the demand for your current products or services in five years' time?
- If you realize there will be a smaller demand, what are you going to do about it today?
- If a larger demand, what are you going to do about it tomorrow?
- Where will you be in 10 years' time? Same house? Same income? Same country?

- If...
  - a manager, do you intend to be in the same job in five years' time? If not, what would you like to be doing? Move up a level? Gain a place on the board? Become the boss?
  - a manager, do you envisage department or team growth or decline?
  - a sole or micro-enterprise and you took on a team of 'associates' who would you need? What difference would this make?
  - you made the time to design a new product or service what would it be?
  - you had more employees, what could be achieved?
  - you personally had more time, what could be achieved?

Glossary

Annum
The phrase 'per annum' means each year, and 'annually' means once every year.

Brainstorming
Brainstorming is explained in the 'Enterprise skills booster' section of Chapter 13, 'Creative thinking'. It is a method of generating new ideas or solutions to problems. The activity is usually a group exercise, though it is possible to brainstorm on your own.

Buyer
A 'buyer' works on behalf of the 'owner' of retail outlets, visiting suppliers and trade fairs to source goods. Often the 'buyer' has the authority to make decisions about whether to place an order. However, sometimes this is not the case. The buyer may have to check with a senior manager or the 'owner' of the business, before going ahead and purchasing products.

Company (limited by guarantee)
The more usual route for a not-for-profit business, such as cultural, ecological, or community organizations, is to incorporate as a Company Limited by Guarantee. This type of company does not have shares or shareholders – it has members instead.

Company (private limited: Ltd)
This is a business structure where the owners of the company are the shareholders and on most occasions company directors. When setting up a private company as 'a director', you become an 'employee' of the company. As shareholders, directors can draw a salary and share dividends/profits, but they cannot sell shares to the public, ie float the business on the stock exchange. To do this they will need to convert to a public limited company (PLC).

Company (public limited: PLC; CPT in Ireland, CCC in Wales)

PLCs (public limited companies) differ from private limited companies in that they are allowed to offer shares to the public to raise funds. Each PLC must have at least two directors to make management decisions, and a company secretary.

Income tax

This is a tax on employee salaries and the profits that a UK self-employed person or partnership makes. (UK companies pay corporation tax on their profits.) In the majority of the states in the United States and elsewhere in the world, income tax is similarly levied against employees and businesses.

Large firm

A large firm is a business, usually in the form of a private or public company, with over 250 employees earning over €50 million per year.

Micro-enterprise

This is a recognized term to describe a business such as a partnership, co-operative or company that has fewer than 10 employees and earns below €2 million per year.

Owner

An owner is someone who owns a business, such as a chain of shops. If you meet with an 'owner' then they can instantly make decisions about whether they are interested in buying from you, usually without the need to consult with others.

Runner

A 'runner' is a person who works on behalf of a 'buyer'. Their usual duties are visiting stands at fairs that buyers do not have time to visit themselves. Runners have no decision powers regarding placing an order. However, they can be impressed by being treated as if they were indeed 'buyers'. If approached by a 'runner' make sure you provide as much information, samples, wholesale/retail price lists and brochures as possible. The runner can then give a good impression of your products to the 'buyer'. Buyers will get back in touch with you if they are interested in placing an order.

Small business

This is a recognized term to describe a business that has fewer than 50 employees and earns less than €10 million per year.

Sole enterprise

The term is used in this book to describe a business managed by one person, eg a sole trader (self-employed) or a sole-director company.

Team-enterprise
This is a term used in this book to describe a business managed by several people, eg a micro-enterprise or small business in the form of a private company, not-for-profit company, partnership or co-operative.

VAT – Value Added Tax
Some businesses opt to register with the Revenue and charge VAT on the sale of their good and services, and many are forced to register when turnover reaches a set threshold. Once registered for VAT, they have to charge VAT on sales, but can claim back VAT on most business expenses.

Some categories of goods and services have different VAT rates and a number of products have a reduced rate of VAT or are exempt. VAT is not a constant percentage across the globe and each country has a different rate that varies between 5 and 25 per cent.

Further reading

Allen, Paul (2007) *Your Ethical Business: How to plan, start and succeed in a company with a conscience,* Ngo Media, London

Arden, Paul (2003) *It's Not How Good You Are, It's How Good You Want to Be,* Phaidon Press, London

Arden, Paul (2006) *Whatever You Think Think The Opposite*, Penguin, London

Austen, Pam and Austen, Bob (2004) *Getting Free Publicity,* How To Books, Oxford

Barrow, Colin (2008) *Starting a Business from Home: Choosing a business, getting online, reaching your market and making a profit*, Kogan Page, London

Beckwith, Harry (2001) *Selling the Invisible: A field guide to modern marketing,* Texere, New York

Berry, Cicely (2000) *Your Voice and How To Use It,* Virgin, London

Binks, Martin and Lumsdaine Edward, (2007) *Entrepreneurship from Creativity to Innovation,* Trafford, Oxford

Borkowski, Mark (2000) *Improperganda: The art of the publicity stunt*, Vision On, London

Boulden, George P (2002) *Thinking Creatively,* (Essential Managers) Dorling Kindersley, London

Buzan, Tony and Buzan, Barry (2006) *The Mind Map® Book,* 2nd edn, BBC Active, Essex

Carnegie, Dale (1998a) *How to Develop Self-Confidence and Influence People by Public Speaking,* 2nd edn, Vermillion, London

Carnegie, Dale (1998b) *How To Win Friends and Influence People,* 2nd edn, Vermillion, London

Charvet, S H (1997) *Words That Change Minds,* 2nd edn, Kendall/Hunt, Iowa

Covey, Stephen R (1999) *The Seven Habits of Highly Effective People,* Simon & Schuster, London

Covey, Stephen R, Merrill, A R and Merrill, R R (2002) *First Things First,* Pocket Books, London

Cushway, Barry (2008) *The Employer's Handbook: An essential guide to employment law, personnel policies and procedures,* 6th edn, Kogan Page, London

Dignen, Shelia (ed) (2000) *Longman Business English Dictionary,* Pearson Education, Essex

Drucker, Peter F and Maciariello, Joseph A (2005) *The Daily Drucker,* Elsevier Butterworth-Heinemann, Oxford

Dyson, James (2002) *Against The Odds: An autobiography,* Texere, New York

Greenfield, Susan (2004) *Tomorrow's People,* Penguin, London

Goldstein, Noah J, Martin, Steve J and Cialdini, Robert B (2007) *Yes! 50 Secrets From the Science of Persuasion,* Chapter 42, What can batting practice tell us about persuasion, Profile Books, London

Goltz, Jay (1998) *The Street-Smart Entrepreneur,* Addicus Books, Nebraska

Hill, Napoleon (2007) *Master Key to Riches,* 2nd edn, Vermillion, London

Hindle, Tim (1998) *Making Presentations,* (Essential Managers) Dorling Kindersley, London

Kao, John J (1989) *Entrepreneurship, Creativity, and Organization,* Prentice Hall, New Jersey

Kennedy, Jamie (2004) *Wannabe,* Aurum Press, London

King, Stephen, Macklin, Jeff and West, Chris (2008) *Finance on a Beermat,* 2nd edn, Random House, London

Love, Sara (ed) (2003) *Handbook: Pricing and ethical guidelines,* 11th edn, The Graphic Artists Guild, New York

Magnus, Sharon M (2003) *Think Yourself Rich,* Vermillion, London

Mariotti, Steve (2000) *The Young Entrepreneur's Guide to Starting and Running a Business,* Three Rivers Press, New York

Mind Gym (2005) *The Mind Gym: Wake up your mind,* Time Warner, London

Moskowitz, Debbie (2007) Judgement days, *Work, Guardian,* 14 July, pp 1–2

Pease, Allan and Pease, Barbara (2004) *The Definitive Book of Body Language,* Orion Books, London

Portas, Mary (2007) *How To Shop with Mary Queen of Shops,* BBC Books, London

Rogers, Carl R (1954) Towards a Theory of Creativity, *A Review of General Semantics,* 11 (4), pp 249–60

Southon, Mike and West, Chris (2002) *The Beermat Entrepreneur,* Pearson, Harlow

Stern, Simon (2008) *The Illustrator's Guide to Law and Business Practice,* Association of Illustrators, London

Sugar, Alan (2005) *The Apprentice: How to get hired,* BBC Books, London

Wind, Yoram Jerry, Crook, Colin and Gunther, Robert (2005) *The Power of Impossible Thinking,* Wharton School Publishing, New Jersey

Wiseman, Richard (2004a) *Did You Spot The Gorilla?* Arrow Books, London

Wiseman, Richard (2004b) *The Luck Factor,* Arrow Books, London